Raising Our Vibrations for the New Age

by Sherri Cortland, ND

OZARK MOUNTAIN PUBLISHING

PO Box 754, Huntsville, AR 72740

800-935-0045 or 479-738-2348; fax 479-738-2448

www.ozarkmt.com

D1042732

For permission, serialization, condensation, adaptions, or for our catalog of other publications, write to Ozark Mountain Publishing, Inc., P.O. Box 754, Huntsville, AR 72740, ATTN: Permissions Department.

Library of Congress Cataloging-in-Publication Data
Cortland, Sherri, 1957 -
   Raising Our Vibrations for the New Age, by Sherri Cortland
How to raise our vibrations to be able to shift with the planet into the next dimension.

1. 2012   2. Ascension   3. Planetary Evolution   4. Automatic Writing
5. Metaphysics
I. Cortland, Sherri, 1957-   II. Human & Planetary Ascension
IV. Metaphysics IV. Title

Library of Congress Catalog Card Number: 2011928006
ISBN: 978-1-886940-18-5

Cover Art and Layout: www.noir33.com
Book set in: Times New Roman
Book Design: Julia Degan

Published by:

OZARK
MOUNTAIN
PUBLISHING
PO Box 754
Huntsville, AR 72740

WWW.OZARKMT.COM
Printed in the United States of America

Rave Reviews for
Raising Our Vibrations for the New Age

"*Raising Our Vibrations for the New Age* provides a clear and concise description of the Shift and all of the important patterns that will take place in our society. Ms. Cortland does a beautiful job explaining what the Shift entails, as well as the many new and remarkable planetary lessons that will evolve from it. This includes everything from how to accept the pattern changes around us to naturopathy. This book will assure that the novice has an understanding of what will happen while it also offers some fresh and thoughtful lessons for the more advanced Lightworker. I highly recommend this book."
Justine Alessi, author of *Rebirth of the Oracle: Tarot for the Modern World*

"Throughout my reading of Sherri Cortland's book, *Raising Your Vibrations for the New Age*, I had a perpetual smile on my face. This was not only because Sherri tells us that smiling is the single most important thing we can do to raise our vibrations but also because what she shares in this book resonated deep within my heart and greatly added to my excitement regarding where we are headed! I cannot recommend this book strongly enough for all of you who want essential information that will help you understand our future and how to prepare for and utilize the many tools available for this Shift. Sherri's book is for all Lightworkers, as well as those still questioning whether the new age is truly upon us. This author has the courage to talk about things we aren't talking about but should be. She has the intelligence to question some long-held beliefs that need to be reevaluated. She has the heart to do everything in her power to help humanity Shift into a new earth as easily as possible, and her genuine enthusiasm is absolutely contagious. Sherri is a clear and responsible channel who is bringing vital and divine information forth to help us all. I hope you read it for yourself, and then I'll bet you'll find yourself smiling, too!"

Mary Soliel, author of *Michael's Clarion Call* and *I Can See Clearly Now: How Synchronicity Illuminates Our Lives*

"A fascinating guide into how to live through upcoming spiritual & global shifts. Easy to read, interesting, and useful."
Alice Grist, author of *The High Heeled Guide to Spiritual Living* and *The High Heeled Guide to Enlightenment* www.alicegrist.co.uk

"Via stunningly authentic, clear connections with her guides and enhanced by her own breathtaking intuitive wisdom and profound spiritual insights, author Sherri Cortland *offers answers to our questions about the shifts rocking our lives.* Sherri's information and writing is so powerful that *I experienced healing at the moment I read* it—*before* even putting anything into practice! The author offers simple step-by-step strategies to help her readers move forward with the *Shift! If you desire to restore your equilibrium and progress instead of getting stuck, Raising Our Vibrations for the New Age* is a vital how-to and must-have!"
Irene Lucas, author of Thirty Miracles in Thirty Days

"Sherri Cortland has a multidimensional wisdom that transcends current perspectives. Her ability to capture this wisdom in the physicality of words and share it in a clear and easy-to-read manner is her grace. To this day, I continue to refer to her book *Windows of Opportunity* regularly. I am thrilled to have access to more of Sherri's wisdom in *Raising Our Vibrations for the New Age*. Having such guidance, I embrace life on new earth with open arms."

Jennifer Crews, M.A. Self-Evolution Expert and author of "Understanding the New Children" (Chapter 26 in *Power of the Magdalene*)

"There have only been a few people in my life that I have instantly recognized as having an infinite connection to the grace-filled, flowing link of divine spirit. Sherri Cortland is such a person. Not only is she deeply connected spiritually, but she is one of the sweetest, most loving persons I have ever met. Her intent to bring you the HIGHEST spiritual TRUTHS through her new book–*Raising Our Vibrations for the New Age*--springs from her innate integrity as she shares her ability to walk between our waking life and the world of eternal secrets that intrigue us all."

Sharry Edwards, Founder and Innovator of Human BioAcoustics

"Jeremy...Gilbert...how come I never get a guide with some big fancy schmancy name?" Fortunately for me, my Guides all have a great sense of humor, and Gilbert was quick to call me on my comment—although he never did tell me what *my* "real name" is!

Gilbert and the Group quickly got started with their dictation and directions regarding what they wanted included in this book; and the purpose of this book was made very clear at the beginning of the dictation process. . .

"The purpose of this book is simple. It is to help people make it through the Shift with as little stress and drama as is humanly possible during a sensation of this type, and it is sensational as it is something that beings are gathering from all corners of the universe to see. It is something that entities would give their "soul teeth" to be part of because it is so juicy and so new and so historic. Being on your side and having to worry about weather changes and storms and disasters isn't fun, and we all know that, but on this side we know that every one of you who is there signed up for it and you were chosen to be there. It is not something that you are part of because of bad luck."

In *Windows of Opportunity*, the Guide Group dictated information to help us get through our daily lives with less drama and less pain. They did this through the introduction of two main concepts: "windows of opportunity" and "relationship villains," and a review of these concepts is in Section One.

For this book, Gilbert and the Group have dictated information that will help us prepare ourselves vibrationally as we journey toward the completion of the Shift, which will, in turn, assist our beloved planet Earth to increase her vibrational level, as well. This is something that we can do with just a little bit of effort as we train ourselves to attract and hold more

INTRODUCTION

It seems like just yesterday that a group of entities on the other side of the veil came together for the specific purpose of dictating material through automatic writing for what became my first book, "*Windows of Opportunity.*" That Guide Group, or the "GG" as I call them, included several of my personal guides, a couple of other entities that I've done automatic writing with in the past, *and* some of my relatives who are currently on the other side of the veil. In fact, my Grandma Knapp acted as "Spokes Guide" for that project!

When Jeremy, the lead guide from the "GG" told me it was time to write *this* book, I fully expected that I would be working with the same group, but that was not the case. A new Guide, Gilbert, is the Spokes Guide for the channeled material presented here. I say my *"new"* Guide," but according to Gilbert, we have worked together many times before, as he reminded me on the day that we began working on *Vibrations*:

> *"Good morning, Sherri, this is Gilbert. We've been waiting for you so let us get to work right away. First of all, Sherri, let me tell you that we have worked together often--you should be feeling my energy right now and you should feel safe and familiar with it. You and I are a team and even though you wish I had a fancy schmancy name, your real name is not so fancy schmancy either!"*

The first time Gilbert came through was a few days before I started channeling new material for this book. I had just sat down at my computer and initiated an automatic writing session with a prayer of protection followed by the words, "Will someone please write with me?" Instead of the usual greeting from the "GG," Gilbert introduced himself to me. Now, about Gilbert's name--not only did I think it, but I laughingly said out loud to my friend, Heidi Winkler,

i

Section Ten: After the Shift

Section Eleven: Opening up to Spirit

Section Twelve: Ready for Action

Section Five: Our Galactic Heritage

Section Six: The Transition

Section Seven: Raising our Vibrations

Section Eight: What We Eat Matters

Section Nine: Alternative Medicine

Table of Contents

Introduction

Section One: Accelerating Spiritual Growth

Section Two: The Shift and Our Role in it

Section Three: Our Atlantean Connection

Section Four: 2012

Christie Czajkowski, Debi Marcocchi, Jenny Oney, Steve Trask, Viki Vertel, and Tina Wolpow. Thanks to you, this book makes sense.

Thank you to Heidi Winkler, Mary Soliel, Shelly Wilson, Steve Trask, and Barbara Byrd for reviewing early drafts and providing me with excellent suggestions, insights, and grammatical corrections to make this book much more readable. Your hard work will never be forgotten—and, I owe you one!

Thank you to Neil Whitehouse. Your words during that never-to-be forgotten lunch helped set the stage for my personal on-going search for the truth. Without you I might still be looking at the world with "James Joycean eyes."

Thank you to all my dear friends (new and old) and my family for their continued love and support, and most especially for not thinking I should be locked up! This list includes but is by no means limited to Maxine Andert, Mike Andert, Debbie Amico, Aby Benjamin, John Brennan, Sue Brennan, Doug Burket, Linda Conklin, Janet Collins, Kathey Condon, Craig Costello, Nicole Georgi-Costello, Diane Diaz, Steve Grecco, Tracy Harman, Leigh Herr, Kim Hoffman, Lori Kelly, Connie Kingery, Shelly Koehler, Sandra Knapp, Lauren Ihburg, Keith Ihburg, Denise Isseks, Terri Marinaro, Marie Mariani, Peggy McGrath, Penny Peppers, Kathy Seeley, Samantha Seeley, Larry Shirley, Rhonda Shirley, Bill Smith, Debbie Smith, Jeff Smith, Debra Thomas and Grace Velez.

And of course, a huge thank you to the fabulously talented staff (especially Dolores, Julia, Joy, and IteRa) at Ozark Mountain Publishing for all the help, wisdom, and advice you continually provide.

This book is dedicated to these incredible beings!

All Lightworkers & Starseeds.
Stay awake! We ARE making a difference!

Ted Dylewski (aka "Teddy-Mac"),
My husband, friend, and partner through the ages.

Marjorie Knapp Ihburg,
My mother, advisor, and counselor in this and many
lifetimes.

Sunna Rasch,
My mentor and inspiration in this and many lifetimes.

Heidi Winkler,
My best friend, confidante, and "rock" through many
incarnations.

Acknowledgements:

Thank you to all my Guides, Angels, and relatives on the other side for your extreme patience and sense of humor during the writing of this book. "Vibrations" would not have been written without the constant nudging and channeled writings of the original GG, Gilbert and the Group, and Akhnanda and the Arcturians. I am grateful to have the honor of working with each of them.

Thank you to Kiernan Antares, Rosemary Gladstar, Irene Lucas, and Nikki Patillo for contributing to the content of this book and/or allowing me to use information from your wonderful books. This book is so much better because of your generosity.

Thank you to all the brave and wonderful Lightworkers and friends who shared your stories with me and allowed me to include parts of your journey in the following pages: Pam Bajaj, Dawn (aka Dawnifer!) Burket, light, and create positive energy. As you will see as you read this book, there is no big, involved, or "fancy schmancy" New Age plan to bring in and hold the light; and the key is simple: To become aware of the consequences of our words, thoughts, and actions. Becoming aware is a giant step toward understanding the consequences of our thoughts, words, and actions, and this awareness will help us wake up to our power. We are all very powerful beings, and we are all able to take control of our thoughts, words, and actions--which means that we can make the *choice* to think, speak, and react *positively* instead of negatively. And that, as you will see, is a very big deal when it comes to (1) raising our personal vibrational levels, (2) raising the vibrational level of the planet, (3) creating positive energy, and (4) bringing and holding the light which will make the Shift less dramatic.

And isn't it interesting to know that we've all chosen to be here at this time to take part in the Shift? We asked to be here and/or we were chosen to take part in this momentous time in history! We learned from the Guide Group in "Windows of Opportunity" that we plan our lives (the good stuff and the bad) in order to learn lessons, have life experiences, and work out Karma. This means that we each have a great responsibility, to each other and to our planet, to do everything we possibly can to bring and hold the light. Each one of us is a lighthouse for the output of positive energy.

I know that in his opening dictation, Gilbert mentioned entities watching what is happening here on Earth. Don't worry about beings from other planets, dimensions, or anyone who is on the periphery to watch the "greatest show in the universe"—if you are reading this book, you are an integral part of attracting and holding light, and that is what we need to concentrate on. Each of us has great power individually, and together we will raise the vibrational level of our beloved planet and make our evolutionary journey easier for everyone.

SECTION ONE:

Accelerating Spiritual Growth

Chapter One:

Windows of Opportunity & Relationship Villains

If you could take control of your spiritual growth and learn your lessons with less drama and pain, would you do it? If you could accelerate your spiritual growth and get through your lessons faster and easier, even if it meant taking a good, hard look at your life and making changes in your behavior where necessary, would you do it?

Our spiritual progress depends on us—we are responsible for our learning and growth, and being the very smart entities that we are, we've made sure that we have the tools to do the job. We've formulated intricate plans and back-up plans, and back-up back–up plans to make sure that we eventually learn our lessons. Becoming aware of these plans and becoming aware of the tools we've provided for ourselves are the first steps toward learning our lessons faster and with less drama and pain, while at the same time making it possible for us to cross lessons off of our To Do Lists at an accelerated rate.

These tools are called Windows of Opportunity and Relationship Villains, two concepts which were originally introduced when the book *Windows of Opportunity* came out in October 2009, and you can read much more about them in that book. For this book, a general understanding of them is necessary, so before we get into the new stuff, let's do a quick review of what our Windows and Relationship Villains are all about.

Windows of Opportunity

Windows are opportunities for growth and learning that we personally designed and created for ourselves while we were on the other side of the veil planning our present incarnation. Think of your life as a book with chapters, and in each chapter we insert scenarios or situations constructed to help us learn a particular lesson or have a growth experience.

Why look for Windows of Opportunity? Each time we learn a lesson or complete an experience on our To Do List for this lifetime, we have more time to work on other items on our learning list. The more we accomplish, the more rapidly we mature spiritually. To make sure that we learn a particular lesson that we are intent on learning, we incorporate many possible Windows of Opportunity into our lives so that if we miss one, we will have another chance to acquire the learning or have the experience we need and want for our spiritual growth. As we miss one window and go on to another, the windows become increasingly more dramatic. Why? To help us wake up and learn our lessons.

Learning to spot windows is like learning any other skill—it just takes practice! Windows are everywhere—at home, at work, even at the grocery store. The best way to find your windows is to examine your life and look for patterns and life scripts. Here's a three-step plan to help you get started.

Step One: Examine your past; it can be a little painful, but it's the best way to begin noticing patterns and scripts.

Step Two: Pay more attention to what's going on *now*. As John Lennon said, "Life is what happens when you're busy making other plans." And as you pay attention to what's going on in the present, go into your memory bank

4

and determine if you had any similar situations or experiences in your past.

Step Three: As you find the patterns and scripts and connect the dots between the past and the present, be honest with yourself. Is there something you can change about your behavior or the way you've handled *like* situations? If a situation keeps repeating, that's an indicator that you need to change how you deal with it. Changing your behavior will help you go through the window and stop the pattern from repeating in the future.

It's very easy for me to sit here, take the dictation, and write the book; it's much harder for me, and all of us, to incorporate these suggestions and action plans from the Guide Groups into our daily lives. But to learn our lessons and, more importantly, to actually *expedite* our spiritual growth, we have to take action—and the more we work on it, the easier it will become. In mid-2009, my cousin, Tracy Costa, introduced me to a friend of hers, Steve Trask. Steve and I quickly hit it off. He was one of the first to read *Windows of Opportunity*, and he shared the following with me in an e-mail about buckling down and doing the work necessary to move ahead. (Note: names have been changed to protect the Relationship Villains involved in this lesson!)

I was tested this evening. My friend Mike planned an evening of dinner and a play, and I offered to have drinks at my house beforehand. Mike, who is always late (which annoys me), called saying he had lost track of time, and so I found myself stuck waiting for him at my house with another friend and his friend, James. I've known James for a while, and he

5

continually irritated me by interrupting everything I tried to say. I was 'over it,' as we would say. All throughout the play I kept thinking (thanks to your teachings and others) that this was a lesson, and wondering what I was supposed to learn. It was tough. I was still irritated, but I knew it was a reflection of an aspect of me, and I needed to work on being less rigid and judgmental. I'm going to have to sleep on this, but I think I know that I need to be more tolerant of others.

Irritated as he may have been, Steve recognized a window and he was doing the work necessary to walk through it. He was looking at situations and trying to figure out if they were script-like, and then looking for ways to change his behavior. Whether he realized it or not when he wrote this e-mail, he was following the action plan outlined above, and I think he'll agree with me that's it's not fun to analyze your own behavior.

Lightworker Tina Wolpow, of Longwood, Florida, has also shared with me several stories that are similar to what Steve wrote about in his e-mail. She's been very busy examining and re-examining situations that have occurred and re-occurred in her life so she can spot her life scripts and put an end to them. The action plan outlined above is work, no doubt about it, and Steve and Tina will back me up on that statement, but it's also an excellent way to figure out our lessons so we can learn them and move forward.

It becomes easier and easier to spot windows once you're aware that they exist and you start looking for them, but you know what's even easier? Spotting someone else's life script! I can tell you all about the scripts that my friends and family are living, but it takes much longer for me to spot my own! It's one of life's little ironies, but it's so true. Maybe we should ask a couple of the people that we love and trust the most if we have any scripts that need attention? It won't be easy to hear the answer, and we'll probably say, "I do NOT do that!" immediately after someone shares a possible script with us, but in the end we'll have some insight into what we need to work on so we can spot our windows closer to the ground floor.

Speaking of the ground floor, during a recent workshop someone voiced the question that I'm sure is on everyone's mind, "How can we spot a window on the ground floor?" That is a difficult question to answer because if we get it right, we might never realize it was a lesson learned. Here are my thoughts on spotting windows on or close to the ground floor:

- If we experience a difficult or challenging situation and it doesn't repeat itself, then we've gone through the window on the ground floor.

- We may not realize it was a window because it was something that came up, we dealt with it properly, learned the lesson, and now we're done with it.

- By paying attention to what's going on in our lives, we'll notice if a similar situation happens again, and hopefully we'll connect the dots, change our behavior, and nip the life script in the bud so we don't have to deal with the same lesson a third, fourth, or fifth time. In this way, we can go through the window while we're still very close to the ground floor.

- If a similar situation pops up a third time, we should be awake enough to realize that we have a life script happening and take the appropriate actions of analyzing and changing our behavior. We're still learning our lesson on a lower floor and saving ourselves from whatever "penthouse" drama we may have planned to shake ourselves awake.

It all comes back to this: each time we go through a window, we are learning a lesson and expediting our spiritual growth—the sooner we recognize a lesson, the faster we go through the window and on to the next item on our To Do List.

Relationship Villains

Relationship Villains are entities that are our closest universal friends when we are on the other side of the veil, but for this incarnation, they have volunteered to play the part of *the bad guy* to help us cross something important off of our spiritual *must learn* list for this incarnation. They might be people who simply annoy us, or even those we consider to be our so-called enemies. They create (or co-create) unpleasant, and even tragic, situations that open Windows of Opportunity for us to learn and grow, or they may take action that forces us to stay on our chosen path. Either way, their purpose is to help us accomplish our learning/growth faster or in what may ultimately be a less dramatic or painful way. Relationship Villains can be anyone; you will find them everywhere. Look for them especially in romantic relationships, family relationships, and work relationships; however, they will also turn up at school, at the grocery store, at the airport, the DMV, and anywhere we happen to be! They can be someone we have an ongoing relationship with or someone we interact with just once or twice. When we learn the lesson, the relationship with our Relationship Villain will become much more palatable (this is usually the case when the Villain is a family member), or the relationship will end because the mission you worked on together is over (as often happens with friends). By the way, just as others act as Relationship Villains to help us, we return the favor. We can have Relationship Villains in our lives and be a Relationship Villain for others during the same incarnation.

Being aware of the Relationship Villain concept is a big first step towards spotting the Villains in our lives. Remember the annoying James mentioned in Steve's story in the "Windows" section? Classic Relationship Villain. James irritated Steve right into realizing what he needs to work on to move ahead, and Steve was awake enough to realize it.

Here's another Relationship Villain experience: in February 2010, Lightworker Debie Marcocchi of Bartlett, Illinois, wrote to share an experience where she suddenly realized that the person being a pain in her neck essentially pushed her to change direction and move forward faster than she thought was possible.

> *Thanks to your book I was able to see a Villain in my life, and she opened a window of opportunity for me. My business partner and I had made an agreement regarding the dissolution of our partnership, and then she changed the terms of our 'exit agreement' and insisted that I had to be out by April 1ˢᵗ. I was very mad about this because her reasoning for this made no sense at all, and her arguments were quite lame! And then it hit me like a ton of bricks! I had been saying over and over again that I wanted to 'be out of there' by April 1ˢᵗ, but I didn't think it was possible. Anyway, I got my wish, thanks to my difficult ex-partner. All of a sudden it dawned on me that she was a Relationship Villain pushing me to move forward with my new career plan.*

Debie had the grand opening of her Free to be Me Wellness Spa and Salon in Bloomingdale, Illinois, on August 1, 2010, and says that her ex-partner helped her step up her

9

schedule by being so difficult and mean. Debie's experience is also a perfect example of why we have to watch what we think and say, which you'll no doubt notice is a repeating theme throughout this book.

I had an experience similar to Debie's, and it also revolved around a Relationship Villain and how powerful our words and thoughts are. The person who cut my hair moved, and we all know how hard it is to find someone that we trust with our hair. I started going to a salon down the street from my house, but the person doing my hair just wasn't understanding what I wanted, and so I was continually thinking and saying that I wanted to find a new hairdresser, but I didn't take any action to make it happen. Two days before I was due to speak at the 2009 Transformations Conference, my first really big speech as an author, I stopped in at my salon for a trim—I wanted to look good up on stage. I stated the importance of just trimming my bangs the tinniest bit and shaping them, and I ended up with zig-zag bangs going across the middle of my forehead. I called my pal Heidi, and as I was crying my eyes out over how bad I looked and what was I going to do, she told me to drive around and find a spa. A spa? I didn't need a facial; I needed new bangs!

Then Heidi explained, "Find a spa to see if you can get a weave on your bangs."

There's an example of thinking outside the box! At that moment of desperation, a "bang weave" sounded almost plausible to me, and just as those words came out of her mouth, I turned the corner, and there was The Fountains Salon & Spa.

I parked my car, tried to suck it up, and be nonchalant about how I looked, but as soon as I walked in the door, I started crying again and said, "I (sob) have (sob) to (sob) give (sob) a speech in two days! Can you (sob) give me a weave (sob) for my bangs (sob)"?

10

Among the many lessons of the day, I learned that you can't just walk in off the street for a weave, but the owner of the salon, Diana Kim, took pity on me and worked a miracle by somehow creating new bangs to cover the Frankenstein mess, and my hair looked great for my big day. I know. Believe me, I know that I overreacted to the bang disaster that day (although, if you saw the picture I took of them, I think you would cry, too!), but that Relationship Villain who destroyed my bangs allowed me to find a great new hairdresser just like I had been wishing for. I had an important reminder about just how powerful our words and thoughts are and how we make things happen.

Since Relationship Villains are catalysts for opening Windows of Opportunity throughout our lives, we look for them the same we look for Windows of Opportunity—by searching for patterns and life scripts. Here are some tips to help you get started.

Keys to Spotting Relationship Villains in Your Life at the Present Time

- Are you involved in on-going arguments or unpleasant situations that are continually caused by the same person? If "Yes," that person is probably a Relationship Villain working very hard to help you learn a lesson. Consider the circumstances and look for patterns to help you figure out your lesson.

- If you are involved in a car accident or someone "does you wrong" at work, it is most likely a Relationship Villain providing you with a Window of Opportunity for growth. How you react to the situation will dictate whether you go through the window or attract a similar circumstance to yourself again in the future.

11

- If someone "bullies" you, he/she is definitely a Relationship Villain and will learn as much from you as you will from him/her. The best way to deal with a bully is to stand up to him/her, learn the lesson, and free yourself to move on to other learning experiences.

How to Spot Relationship Villains from Your Past *and* Keep Them from Appearing in Your Future

- Do a mini-life review and look at situations surrounding people you feel have "done you wrong" and those in your life that you find particularly annoying or whom you might consider to be your enemies. Carefully review the circumstances around your interaction with them and ask yourself these questions:
  - Did I learn anything from my experience with this person?
  - Would things have been different for me if I had handled the situation in another way?

- You may find that the people you think "did you wrong" actually made things better for you in the long run or steered you toward a path that will help you accomplish your lessons faster and more easily.

Relationship Villains are the catalysts that make it possible for our Windows of Opportunity to work, and when we understand and take responsibility for the creation of our windows, it becomes easier and easier for us to forgive the Villains in our lives. Forgiving our Villains helps us let go of old wounds and negative energy so that we can move forward with our lives and expedite our spiritual growth.

Chapter Two:

Becoming Aware

In preparation for our present incarnation, we created a blueprint or plan of action that incorporates all the lessons and life experiences necessary for us to accomplish our goals for this lifetime. Next we constructed our Windows of Opportunity (the *how* part of our experiences), and then we made agreements regarding who would be our family, friends, and even our Relationship Villains (the *who* part of our experiences).

We planned our experiences based on specific goals, and we surrounded ourselves with entities who agreed to help us accomplish these goals. We all play many different roles during an incarnation, and we all help each other learn and grow.

According to the GG, the people that annoy or antagonize us, those that we may not like or who have caused trouble or even tragedy for us, are most likely our closest universal friends. Relationship Villains are entities that love us enough to play a villain role so that we can learn a lesson or have an experience that we very much want to have. Playing a villain role is something that entities do out of love and friendship for each other because it's always a sacrifice. It's easy to play the good guy but much harder to put on the black hat and play the role of the bad guy. Yet we need these so-called bad guys to help us learn and grow. Our Relationship Villains are very much the *catalysts* for our various learning experiences.

The GG also say that as we begin to accept our role in planning the *good* **and** the *bad* things that happen to us, like car accidents, for example, we'll be that much more awake when it comes to being on the lookout for our Windows of Opportunity. Taking responsibility for what happens to us will also help us expedite our growth because we'll forgive ourselves and others faster, thus enabling us to move forward more rapidly.

When it comes to our windows, the GG likes to say that it's better (and certainly *easier*) for us to learn the lesson on the ground floor rather than in the penthouse—and who would argue with this logic? Learning to spot our Windows of Opportunity closer to the ground floor not only helps us work through our lessons faster and with less drama and pain, it also helps us to expedite our spiritual growth and raise our vibrations because we will achieve more in less time.

I've been *Window watching* for a couple of years now, and I can tell you that it gets easier and easier to spot them as you go along. It's definitely a skill that's developed over time, but it takes being aware of what's going in your life and being honest with yourself (which is not always pretty or easy!) about what's going on in your life. To start honing this skill, examine what's going on in your life right now. Spot your windows by searching for something that's going on presently that is a repeat of a similar situation you've already lived through once or twice—kind of like a life script. Life scripts are actually a series of Windows of Opportunity where we **didn't** learn the lesson, so we keep attracting similar circumstances to ourselves. By spotting a life script, we can also begin to recognize a lesson (Window of Opportunity) for growth.

So if the same type of situation keeps occurring in your life, that's a clear message that you should examine how you dealt with it in the past, and then change your behavior. Why change your behavior? Because handling the situation the same way you did in the past didn't deliver the desired learning results. Altering how you dealt with similar situations in the past will enable you to go through the Window and stop the pattern from repeating in the future.

SECTION TWO:

The Shift & Our Role in It

Chapter Three:

Exactly What Is the Shift?

It's a **Shift in Consciousness**—for the human race and for the planet Earth. At the same time we are working to facilitate this Shift, we are also dealing with karma and lessons and trying very hard to move forward spiritually. We've got a lot on our plates as we struggle with our day-to-day activities and the challenges and tragedies that are part of our lives as individuals. Add the additional responsibility each of us has assumed to bring in and hold the light and create positive energy to facilitate the Shift, and there you have it—a bunch of very tired human beings! How are we doing so far? Here's a progress report from Gilbert and the Group:

> *From this side* [of the veil] *it is considered great good luck to be part of such a momentous, historic time period because it is like no other in recent history. It is of epic proportions like the Atlantean disasters before. When a civilization undergoes such change as you are currently undergoing, it is a time for great rejoicing because it heralds a change in the vibrational level of the planet.*
>
> *Sometimes such a change is a going backward to start again and try to get it right the next time. Sometimes, like now, it is a going forward, a great movement forward that will help the human race progress. In this case you are progressing like you never have before. An entire race of beings, not just one small group, will move forward. An entire planet will move forward and the universe watches. And the universe waits. This is truly an historic occasion!*

19

And how can this be happening? It happens on the backs or rather the souls of all those who came before, and those who are incarnated right now making it happen. And it happens one soul and one being at a time because without individuals working and helping to bring the light to the planet, none of this would be happening right now.

This is a tribute to the Lightworkers, to the re-born Atlanteans and Lemurians, and to those who have incarnated here from other dimensions and other planets to help bring this grand plan to fruition. And the plan is coming to fruition. On that you can bank your money.

The plan is nearing the end, and we are celebrating. Oh the celebrations that are going on right now are enormous because we can see the flow of the vibrations and the flow of your hard work. By your hard work, we mean the work of all those who are incarnated on the planet right now because none of this would be happening without this exact group of souls doing the work they came here to do. The celebrations will continue as we get closer to finishing the job, and you will all feel great rejoicing and a feeling of great accomplishment for what you have made happen for the human race and for the universe as a whole.

You see, it is not just the planet Earth or the human race that will benefit from these changes. This is a major accomplishment for the entire universe and for all beings because what is being accomplished on Earth has never taken place before—human beings responsible for the change in the level of vibrations for an entire planet. There have been many ups and many downs on this great path, this great experiment, and we have watched and done our part from this side, but this was a job for those of you incarnated on that side—it was left to you to make this happen.

It's great to know that our hard work is paying off because our job here isn't easy. Somewhere between taking care of our karmic debt, learning lessons, and having life experiences, we've managed to help our species evolve, and for that, we do deserve a pat on the back from the other side. But our job isn't finished; we still have work to do. As part of this great happening, this Shift to a higher energy for human beings and for the planet Earth, our job is simple, but it's not easy. We must continue to bring the light to our planet and create positive energy within our third-dimensional world. The better we do our job, the easier the Shift will be. Gilbert will share many painless ways for us to assist each other and the planet in Section Seven.

Something important to keep in the forefront of our minds as we continue on with our lives and our work is that each and every one of us is important, very important, and what we do individually *does* matter and *does* affect the success of our mission. Knowing how important we are individually, just imagine the effect we have on this planet as a group. It is the hope of Gilbert and the Group that through this book, we will utilize our power and focus on creating more and more positive energy every day, which will, in turn, help raise the vibrational level of our species and our planet.

Chapter Four:

Lightworkers

We're all familiar with the term "Lightworker," we've been hearing it for years. But what exactly *is* a Lightworker? To answer this question, I went back to basics, which for me is Doreen Virtue and her book, *A Lightworker's Way*. I took the following definition of a Lightworker directly from Doreen's website at www.angeltherapy.com:

> *Lightworkers are those who volunteered, before birth, to help the planet and its population heal from the effects of fear. Each Lightworker is here for a sacred purpose. Everywhere on the planet right now, Lightworkers are awakening to faint memories about why they came to Earth. They hear an inner calling that can't be ignored. This call is a reminder that it is now time to stop toying with material dreams and get to work. Many Lightworkers are discovering innate spiritual gifts, such as psychic communication skills and spiritual healing abilities. These are the gifts that we volunteered to use to heal the Earth and her population during the crucial decades surrounding the millennium.*

Gilbert and the Group would like to add the following information to Doreen's definition to help round out our understanding of Lightworkers and their mission on planet Earth:

Sherri, to learn and grow on Earth is to make immense progress in a much shorter period of time

23

than to undertake that learning on this side where we are awake, and that is why souls line up to reincarnate on this planet. But there is more occurring on Earth than souls working through their karma. Many millions of people who are currently incarnated are what we call Lightworkers, and many of them are not indigenous to the planet Earth. Whether they have the bulk of their incarnations on Earth or other planets, they are here on a special mission. They were recruited because they are energy specialists, light specialists, and healing specialists.

They are a SWAT team for the dimensional Shift and they are here, costumed as human beings, in order to get the job done. A Lightworker's efforts must happen from within the human race as there is a strict non-interference policy for the planet Earth. Remember, this is a planet of free will, and so the only way to effect change here is for the SWAT team to incarnate on Earth in human bodies and work undercover and within the restrictions of the planet.

How difficult is that? Wouldn't it be easier to just land the ships and say to the world, 'Here is what needs to be done. Let's do it together'?

That can't happen—it would be deemed interference. Having to be undercover is why so many entities are striving to wake up and do the work that needs to be done to facilitate the Shift. Fortunately just by being on the planet, they are drawing and holding the light. As they meet others, there is something about them that stirs something in those they meet, and in that way they help each other to wake up.

Earth is an undercover operation of galactic proportions! It's all about entities touching others and causing one another to stir and realize who they are. Now they may not understand what's going on or

24

even know that they've been touched, but their subconscious knows it, and their Higher Selves are able to assist in that activation as well. It's like turning on a switch.

What Gilbert says here about having to work for change from within the human race is very similar to dictation that I received from Akhnanda, a new guide who will make his debut in Section Five: Our Galactic Heritage. When I think about this idea of "working from within," my thoughts immediately go to the Indigo, Crystal, and Rainbow generations, who are collectively known as the Star Children. I approached leading Star Child authority Nikki Patillo, author of *Children of the Stars* and *A Spiritual Evolution* and boldly asked her if she would help us understand the roles that these Lightworker groups play in our evolutionary process, and she generously and graciously provided the following information:

Defining Star Children

Star children are children who have been sent here from all areas of the universe to help the Earth and the people on it. They possess psychic, spiritual, and other extrasensory abilities. These children will bring peace, topple corrupt systems, and shift dimensional consciousness in the years to come. They have come here on special assignment to assist in this rebirth into a higher dimensional earth.

Star children have been divided into three categories: Indigo, Crystal, and Rainbow. Star children have chosen specific parents who will help them develop their natural abilities. So if you are a parent of a child you know is different, your child probably chose you to help him/her help others on his/her spiritual path. How lucky you are to be the chosen parent of one of these incredibly gifted souls here to help this Earth.

The three groups of children (Indigo, Crystal, and Rainbow) each have a specific task. The Indigo children are here to break down the paradigm of the traditional thinking. Then the Crystal children will build their foundation on the broken paradigm. Finally, the Rainbow children are here to build on what the Indigo and Crystal children have begun.

Indigo Children

Indigo children started arriving during the 1970's and have distinct warrior personalities. They will stand up and fight for what they think is right and what they believe. They also know when they are being lied to and manipulated and will not comply with any system that may be limiting or dysfunctional. Indigos also have little or no tolerance for dishonesty. They are here to show us that the archaic systems in schools, government, parenting, and healthcare are not healthy and must change, or we will continue to fail globally as a civilization. Larger numbers of Indigo children started arriving around 1992. In fact, if your child was born after 1992, there is a good chance you have an Indigo child.

Crystal Children

The Crystal children began to appear on the planet from about 1990-2010 although a few scouts came earlier. Their main purpose is to take us to the next level in our evolution and reveal to us our inner and higher power. They function as a group consciousness rather than as individuals, and they live by the "Law of One" or global oneness. They are also advocates for love and peace on this planet.

Crystal children can also be very high energy, have strong personalities, be creative, and can instantly manifest anything they want or need.

Rainbow Children

The Rainbow children are the third generation of special children that have come to help humanity evolve. Different from the Indigo and Crystal children, Rainbow children have a few more interesting characteristics. The Rainbow children are generally born in the year 2000 and above. In some cases, there might also be a few scouts that came to Earth before 2000. The few Rainbow children that are here today are born from early Crystal scouts that were born in the 1980's. Astonishingly, the Rainbow children come with no karma. Rainbow children will enjoy the life on Earth learning with absolutely no strings attached to their past. This is because they do not really continue from any previous cycle of reincarnation. This is also why they have a very high-energy frequency and physical energy.

There is so much more to read and know about these three Lightworker branches, and I especially recommend Nikki's books to anyone who was born or has a child born in 1990+. Now let's get back to Gilbert and the Group as they continue their discussion about Lightworkers:

Sherri, where is all this work being done? You don't see entities walking, physically bumping into each other, and saying, 'There. I've activated your switch; you're awake. Now get to work!'

It doesn't work like that. Many Lightworkers are writing books, lecturing, channeling, and doing energy work. The word is getting out faster than ever before, which is important because things are changing faster than ever before. Those who are putting themselves on the line may find their reputations suffering slightly with part of society while at the same time they are much welcomed by another section of society who thirsts for the knowledge that will help them wake up and get to work.

Lightworkers are truly working around the clock, and much is learned at night while they are asleep. This is a time that much work is being done as Lightworkers temporarily leave their bodies to commune, discuss, and take action. Soul groups come together at night to focus their combined energies on areas that are important for the Shift of the planet, particularly for the purpose of healing the planet. So much is done during the sleep period, and sometimes Lightworkers' travels and activities are reflected in their dreams. Sometimes they remember bits and pieces, but they often dismiss them.

This last bit of dictation explains why many of us sleep for seven or eight hours and still wake up tired—we've been busy working all night long! The "bits and pieces" of information that we wake up remembering but quickly forget are things that we should record immediately upon awakening in a notebook or journal that we keep on our nightstands. When we leave our bodies, we are essentially astral traveling, and when we do that, we are operating outside of our current third-dimensional energy. As we record our dreams and bits of dreams, we're bringing energy and light into this reality. By writing down what we remember when we first wake up, we're allowing information from our subconscious to enter our conscious mind. While it might just be "bits and pieces" at first, we'll be training ourselves to actively remember our dreams. Someday we'll be able to remember our travels, the work we do at night, and the interaction we have with our soul groups. "Remembering" is another skill that we'll get better at with practice and as our vibrational levels continue to increase.

Chapter Five:

A Message for Lightworkers

(If you're reading this book, this means YOU*!)*

In August 2009, I appeared on my very first radio show, Truthbrigade Radio, talking with host Christie Czajkowski about how we could work together to put more positive energy into the atmosphere. I quoted from a list of actions that was originally included in *Windows of Opportunity*. Christie, who is a very bright light on Earth and has taught me a lot about facing adversity, said to me in the nicest and most polite way, "Sherri, do you really believe that smiling at each other will make a difference?"

I totally understood why she asked me that question; I would have asked the same thing if I were the host. And as naive as this might sound, I *do* believe that even one smile will have a positive effect on multiple people, and the effect of that one smile on those people will also infuse the atmosphere with positive energy. You smile at me and we both feel great. That one smile lifts both our moods, and that smile might be the momentum for countless smiles that we give to others, which they pass on during the rest of the day. The act of smiling exudes positive energy—smiles are infectious, and they are an easy way to create positive energy and share our light with fellow human beings. When we smile, we shine our light, and that, according to Gilbert, is something that we can do more of as we continue to wake up to our mission.

There are many Lightworkers incarnated now that could be doing more—some have dimmed, and this is

31

not the time to be a dim Lightworker. Now is the time for Lightworkers to open their eyes, wake up, and step up to their individual missions so that we can ease the evolution of humankind and the planet to a higher level of consciousness.

The sooner Lightworkers come together, shine, and do their jobs, the easier the transition will be. So ask us, as you should, what are the Lightworkers supposed to be doing? How do they know what they are supposed to be doing? These are such difficult questions to answer as everyone is different with individual missions, but the one thing all Lightworkers have in common and something that is the job of every Lightworker is the responsibility to attract and hold the light. The more light, the easier the transition for the Lightworker, the planet, for those who transition to New Earth, and for those who will not transition at this time. [Note: See Section Ten for more about New Earth and Section Six for more about those who will not transition at this time.]

And how does a lightworker attract and hold the light? By being *of the light, by* acting *as if you are of the light—and that includes making behavioral changes. Certain behavioral changes will not only allow you to learn lessons and accelerate your spiritual growth, they will also help you increase your vibrational level by decreasing the amount of negative energy and increasing the amount of positive energy. Stopping the road rage, stopping the rudeness, and stopping the violence are three very good ways to get started. If each individual takes responsibility for spewing less negativity out into the world, then the world will be a more positive place. The darkness will continue to lift as it's replaced by more and more light. Do you see that each Lightworker can contribute greatly by doing very little?*

This is a subject that is continually dictated about by all three Guide Groups working with me and is continually reinforced in the channeled messages that I receive from the original GG, Gilbert and the Group, and Akhnanda and the Arcturians. The point they continually drive home is that we are powerful beings. Because we aren't fully awake to who we are, we forget our power and our ability to effect great change. This is what we need to wake up to—it's time for us to take responsibility not only for our own spiritual growth but also for the evolution of our species.

When I'm at a sales meeting at work, and the person leading the meeting has us all stand up to do an exercise, I cringe—I hate doing that kind of stuff. And so I apologize upfront for this next part, but I have an exercise from Gilbert for you to try: take a minute right now and think about how many people you interact with and touch during your normal day.

When I did this exercise myself, I was surprised to see how many lives I touch in a single ten-hour day: I found that I speak to a minimum of forty different people every day at my job, and then I interact with at least another 5-10 people doing errands on the way home, i.e., stopping at the grocery store, bank, post office. When I get home, I speak to my husband and my niece, so add them in, and if my neighbors are outside, I talk to them, too! Plus, I talk to friends and other family members on the phone. I also e-mail back and forth each day with my two sisters and my aunt. Each week I e-mail at least 4-5 different family members, other than those I've already mentioned, so I'll add them to the count for the week as a whole. I have a condo that I rent out to tourists for vacations, so I'm speaking to folks about that on the phone each week or e-mailing them with details. I answer people who write to me directly or through my website with questions about material covered in my book or newsletter. And I respond to comments on Facebook and comments left about articles I have on E-Zines, Hubpages, and Selfgrowth.com. It's shocking, isn't it, when you start to count the numbers of lives you touch on a daily and weekly basis?

When you do this exercise, it becomes very clear how many people we each have the opportunity to share our light with during the course of a single day or a single week—and each day/week is different! We touch different people each day as we go about our daily errands, chores, jobs, and just live our lives. In turn, they touch other people. Smiling and being pleasant allows us to share our light and create positive energy; in so doing, we spread the light, and THAT is the number one job of every Lightworker on this planet. And that is an example of the POWER that we all have to make a difference. Speaking of smiling and having the power to make a difference, Gilbert has more for us about the challenges of being a Lightworker:

To be a Lightworker is difficult because you are charged with knowing. All Lightworkers know they are different, and they all know they have something to do. This doesn't necessarily allow them to be a perfect fit with mainstream society. While the subconscious, the Higher Self, is behind the scenes directing many parts of the mission, there is much that can be done consciously by all to bring more light to the planet, and this is accomplished by stopping negative behaviors and promulgating positive energy.

This is a great moment in time and those brave souls who are incarnated on this planet now are here for a reason. They are here to assist the transition and facilitate evolution. As we have told you in the past and because it is so crucial right now, we remind you again—tell all that they must do their part to bring in and share the light. You don't have to be from another planet, galaxy, or universe to bring in and hold the light, and you don't have to be from another dimension to exude positive energy and raise vibrations—everyone on the planet at this time has this power.

When Gilbert talks about the *subconscious* directing us, he is talking about our Higher Selves. We are all expressions of our Higher Selves. We are a piece of our Higher Self incarnated here and now to learn lessons, have life experiences, and for many of us, to be part of the larger mission. It is our Higher Self that knows exactly what our mission is on this planet at this time. Our Higher Self can communicate with us through meditation, and it communicates with us through our subconscious mind. Our Higher Self speaks to us as *that little voice within* that we all know we need to pay more attention to! The more attention we pay to that small voice, the more we will hear it, hopefully pay attention to it, and the easier our lessons will be. Listening to that voice will help us spot our Windows of Opportunity faster and help us learn our lessons with less drama and pain. It will also direct us and keep us on our path. Think of the Higher Self as an internal GPS!

Let's get back to Gilbert and the Group as they continue with dictation regarding ways to quell negativity and increase positive energy and light.

Judging people is a ridiculous pastime as no one on your side of the veil can possibly know what is going on with any one individual or group. The act of choosing to not judge people will go a long way in allowing the light to enter and stay on the planet. We hope we have made this point clear, and we elaborate on it ad infinitum because it is so important.

Again, we tell you that 2012 is not locked in stone. The planet will complete the Shift when the time is right, and until then, there is time for all the people of the world to work together to make this evolution less stressful for everyone.

Let's recap before we move on to the next section. 2012 is not set in stone as the completion date for the Shift [See Section Four], so we should probably not go out and spend every penny we have saved because "The world is going to end in a couple of years." We know that the Shift is already happening, and we know that we have the POWER to make it easier for those making the transition <u>and</u> for those who are choosing not to transition at this time.

Knowing that we have the power to make it an easier transition and *knowing* that we are here as part of a brigade of souls incarnated now not only to work out our own stuff, but to be part of a great mission to help the human species and our planet evolve, we need to ask ourselves this question: Are we willing to step up and do as much as we can to bring more light to this planet and spread that light? THE TIME IS NOW to move from talking about our mission to physically and mentally taking action. And that is what this book is all about—how do we take that action? How do we start attracting more light to ourselves and spreading that light to others around the world? This isn't just about our families or our neighborhoods—it is about our entire planet and our entire species—we are all connected, and together we are about to make universal history. We also now know that we can effect change by simply smiling and being nice to those around us because they are two very easy ways to share the light and radiate positive energy into the atmosphere. Gilbert and the Group have also made it clear that if we stop judging others, we will make room for more light by decreasing the amount of negative energy we release into the atmosphere. In Section Seven, we will get to the nitty gritty "To Do" list of the things we can all do that will help us raise our vibrations for the New Age. And as we put these small steps into practice, we will help raise each other's vibrations and consciousness, as together we enable our planet and humankind to complete this unprecedented Shift and EVOLVE together. That is the power of the human being. THAT is the power of YOU. THAT IS THE POWER OF US.

Chapter Six:

Facing Fear

We all know our planet is going through changes, and we all know that we are at least knee-deep in the Shift and heading for the waist. There's a ton of fear surrounding the Shift and the 2012 date. We continually have to deal with terrorist activities, on-going wars, environmental disasters, and as I write this section, our economy is still in bad shape. All around us our friends and loved ones are going through difficult times. There is no doubt that the challenging times we are living through are scary as well as exciting, but something we all need to remember is that **we signed up to be here now**! We're not living through these times by accident. Everyone who is presently incarnated on planet Earth wanted/agreed to be here. Lightworkers volunteered to be here (and some were no doubt drafted!) and to be born together at precisely the right time in order to wake up and be in position when needed. Remember the first big influx of Lightworkers during our recent history? It was the Flower Children of the 60's! They were followed by the Baby Boomers (whom we now know are reincarnated Atlanteans), then the Indigos, Crystals, and Rainbows, each bringing an evolved energy and awareness to the planet. And there are more generations of Lightworkers on the way. Why are so many different groups of Lightworkers here now at the same time? Because this planet is making universal history—our entire planet, along with its inhabitants, is Shifting *together*—we're in the throes of it as you read these words.

Human Beings are evolving together into something more than we have ever been before, and the Earth is

evolving as well. When the vibrational level of the planet and the vibrational level of human beings reach the correct level, the Shift will be complete, and the planet and her people will remain in sync with one another. It's a thrilling time to be in body and watch such exciting changes happening all around us. But even though we asked to be here, these changes are scary, too, because many of the things that we're used to and familiar with must change. Without such changes we can't progress; we have to change in order to evolve. And change breeds fear because that is the way of life in a third-dimensional modality; however, we can use fear to learn and grow by confronting it and taking control.

Things are changing quickly for everyone on our beautiful planet, and things are changing much more quickly for Lightworkers than for anyone else. Why? Because **Lightworkers are always on the front lines** during times such as these, and it has always been this way. Lightworkers thrive on overcoming adversity and paving the way for great change and great progress. Why else would we continually sign up for this kind of work incarnation after incarnation? This is not our first battle on the field of evolution. **For Lightworkers, the time is NOW to wake up and follow** *that little voice within* because that voice is what will guide you to where you need to be and to what you are here to do in order to facilitate our progress on Earth during this Shift.

There are many roles to play during the Shift and what may seem like a simple job at first glance, may well be one of the most important jobs to be done. So don't be disappointed if the *little voice within* guides you to simply bring in and hold the light in certain places on the globe or asks you to send more positive vibrations to those around you at work and at home by being nicer and smiling more.

Many Lightworkers are already awake and many are currently waking up. Some are moving forward, and some are

40

stagnant because they are afraid of the changes taking place around us. It's much more challenging for us to get our bearings once we're on this side of the veil striving to wake up while dealing with everyday life. Everyday life on planet Earth is hard, and it's so much easier for us to know what to do *before* we pop into our new bodies. When we're sitting at the planning table making our To Do List, we're wide awake and we understand the big picture—we know that all the bumps, bruises, and heartbreaking tragedies have a higher purpose. Unfortunately, we're not born awake to *why* things happen to us once we're in body. Also, once we're back on <u>this</u> side of the veil, we have to deal with something we never have to face on the other side—an extremely strong negative force that we call fear.

Fear gets in our way, and even the most experienced and decorated of Lightworkers has trouble facing the astonishing amount of fear that exists on Earth and is, in fact, churned out into the atmosphere every day of our lives (one example: all the speculation about 2012 being the end of the world). We need to recognize fear for what it is and use it to expedite our spiritual growth. We accomplish this by facing and dealing with our fears. Fear is a negative force that exists on this planet, but it's one that we can extinguish like a campfire at scout camp, *if* we choose to. We can deal with our fears or we can let them control us. It's a conscious choice that we make, and making the **decision** to **face our fears** is a massive step forward if we wish to achieve the following:

- take control of our lives,
- expedite our spiritual growth,
- raise our vibrations,
- **and** keep our feet firmly planted on the evolutionary highway.

Part of *evolving* is recognizing our fear and then dealing with it. Again, dealing with our fears or not dealing with them is a conscious choice that we make, and deciding to face our fears is a massive step forward when it comes to taking control of our lives, expediting our spiritual growth, and utilizing our power.

I think that one of the reasons fear is able to take hold of us the way it does is because the majority of us try to avoid it or deny it instead of facing it head-on. We already know that the universe gives us whatever it is we focus on, so it's no surprise that we must train ourselves to focus on the things we truly want and not on the things we don't want. And now comes the tricky part: by trying to *avoid* what we fear, we end up spending a lot of time thinking about what we fear. Thinking and talking about things is how we communicate with the universe, and **whatever we *dwell upon*, the universe interprets as a message that this is what we want in our lives**. And the universe is going to give it to us! The universe is very generous this way! This is why we have to be careful about what we put out to the universe; for example, we could say that we don't want to be out of a job and then think about nothing else BUT being out of a job, and what do you think the universe will make happen for us? We'll be filing for unemployment insurance in no time because that's what the universe thinks we want.

I've said many times in lectures, articles, and workshops that the GG and Gilbert and the Group want us to know that our thoughts and words are becoming more and more powerful every day. What we think about is what we get—and what we think about is what we draw to ourselves. We can say one thing aloud but think the opposite and guess what we'll end up with? The thoughts of human beings are *that powerful*. Now imagine how powerful we are *together*, and you'll understand how groups like the Flower Children, Baby Boomers, Indigos, etc., can effect such great change.

42

So recognize *your* power, acknowledge that *you* are a powerful being, and then use that power to help yourself overcome your fears. We all have the power to turn fear, which again is a form of negative energy, into positive energy. The more positive energy we generate, the better off we all are. We all have the power, the muscle, and the clout necessary to transmute negative energy into positive energy, and we do it by facing our fears and then letting them go. This is a skill we will improve—just like spotting Windows of Opportunity and life scripts. To help us hone this skill, here's a 4-step plan based on information from Gilbert and the Group:

1. Define exactly what it is that causes you to be afraid. We have to first identify what it is in order to counteract or neutralize it.

2. Once you know exactly what it is you fear, acknowledge it, recognize it, and then release it. Let it go. Make sure you're in touch with the actual related feelings. Acknowledge them and then release those unwanted feelings. Letting go will neutralize it.

3. If you have trouble letting it go—believe me that happens to me every time I face something that evokes fear in me—meditate. Meditate on how to neutralize your fear and then pay attention and listen to that *little voice within.* That little voice is your Higher Self—the part of us that's not incarnated and can still see the big picture and purpose for this incarnation. That little voice is, therefore, in the catbird seat when it comes to giving us guidance.

4. Visualize yourself free from that fear. Visualization is putting your thoughts into action, and taking action is how to handle fear: face it, neutralize it,

and move on. That's how Lightworkers keep fear from blocking the light! That's how we increase our vibrational levels, and that's how we *evolve*.

And please don't allow yourself to get bogged down talking to others who *revel* in their fear/s. Fear is like the common cold. If we're not careful, we can easily pick up someone else's fears, internalize them, become stuck with them ourselves AND then pass them on to others. Some have been afraid so long that their fear is now so familiar and comfortable to them that they aren't really interested in making changes. They just like to talk about what they're afraid of, an act that will only lead to more of the same.

As author Mary Soliel so eloquently writes in her eye-opening book, *I Can See Clearly Now—How Synchronicity Illuminates Our Lives*: ***"When we allow ourselves to get trapped into fear and focus on it, we can actually attract and thus create synchronicity that reflects that fear."*** Mary is right. If we focus on fear, the universe will bring us more of what we fear—it's the way the universe works. Let me close this section with a reminder that no one can face our fears for us. It's something we have to do ourselves. Remember, too, that part of waking up is taking responsibility for moving our lives forward, which has the great side benefit of accelerating spiritual growth. Here's the bottom line when it comes to fear: face it, neutralize it, and move on. That's how we keep fear from getting in the way of our light, that's how we expedite our spiritual growth, and that's how we evolve.

Chapter Seven:

Manifesting 101—Use Your Words Wisely

It doesn't matter which Guide or Guide Group is writing with me, they are all emphatic that we understand the power of our words and thoughts. Frankly, I didn't know how much more I could say about this subject, and then *The Intenders Handbook, a Guide to the Intention Process and the Conscious Community* by Tony Burroughs fell into my hands. This is a short, easy-to-read, and very much to-the-point guide wherein Mr. Burroughs teaches the reader about intent and how to use our words to manifest the things we want (thereby avoiding what we don't want) with much focus on the **clarity** of our words. He talks about the fact that choosing our words carefully and being as exact as possible in our affirmations is key to achieving the desired outcome because choosing the correct words helps us focus our thoughts. We all know how important our thoughts are! Here's an exercise outlining the difference we can make with just a little tweaking of our words.

- "I **want** a new car." (Burroughs: *wanting* indicates a state of lack.)
- "I **hope** I get a new car." (Burroughs: *hoping* indicates doubt that you'll get what you want.)
- "I **intend** that I have a new car." (Burroughs suggests we replace "I want" and "I hope" with *"I intend."* This slight change, though very subtle, has taken the scarcity out of the picture and brought us much closer to our own empowerment.)

A small change in the wording of our thoughts and words as we make an affirmation makes all the difference in helping us manifest the things we want in life. Of course, we must add visualization into our affirmation. Picture yourself in that new car (or whatever it is that you intend for yourself) as you think and say the words, "I intend that I have a new car." Being Lightworkers, we can see how this tweaking of words will impact our personal and planetary evolution as we INTEND healing for our planet, INTEND to shine our light, and INTEND to spot our Windows of Opportunity closer to the ground floor, which brings us to the next part of manifesting.

Knowing how important clarity is and knowing how powerful *you* are, there's one more thing to keep in mind as we discuss the subject of manifesting. We must make sure we stay on track spiritually. In David K. Miller's book, *New Spiritual Technology for Fifth-dimensional Earth,* he channels the following advice from Juliano & the Arcturians:

> *Each of you has come to Earth to learn how to practice and refine this technique of spiritual and mental energy with intention, so that you can manifest, influence, and affect outcomes. You must learn this lesson slowly. For example, if you learned it when you were nineteen years old and used these powers to manifest a million dollars, then that might immediately take you off the spiritual path and might not be in your higher interest.*

So what's a human being to do? We have the power to manifest our desires, but we're not awake enough to know if those desires will take us off track!? There's a little caveat that we can add to our intention statement/affirmation to make sure that we don't upset the To Do List and learning goals we have set for ourselves: "I intend [place your intention here] *if it's for the highest good.*"

No doubt we will start putting our manifesting skills to great use intending nice cars, great jobs, and good hair days, which we all deserve, but let's also use the power of our intentions, the power of our words and thoughts, to help us raise our vibrations; i.e., "I intend that my vibrational level is compatible with the Fifth Dimension," or "I intend that I will spot my Windows of Opportunity early and expedite my spiritual growth." No one said we have to choose between having a great hair day and learning our lessons!

Chapter Eight:

Those Who Will Transition During the Shift

We are **all** here with our own personal agenda and a To Do List of the things we want to accomplish and learn for the purposes of personal spiritual growth, and many of us are also part of the mission to assist Earth and others in their evolution. But, according to my Guide Groups, not everyone currently incarnated on the planet will make the initial transition. If you just did an intake of breath and felt a moment of shock and disappointment, followed by extreme concern, and maybe even shed a tear or two, then you are having some of the same reactions I had when I first received the following information from Gilbert:

> *For some it* [the Shift] *will be a time of great joy, but for many it will initially be a sad time for those who transition with the planet. This is because some entities have chosen to or must complete their lessons in the density and energy of the third dimension. There will be surprises regarding who Shifts and who does not Shift. Now having given you this information, Sherri, we caution you to not allow yourself to look at others and think, 'Will he or will she make it through the Shift?' or 'I don't think that person is going to make it through the Shift.' That kind of thought process is useless and counter-productive. It is each individual entity's business, and no one else's, whether he/she/it transitions or stays.*

49

Not everyone is supposed to transition to the fifth dimension at this time. Some souls are not ready to do this. Their energy levels will not allow it, and they have more to learn before they can make such a transition. This is not something to be judged and talked about. Each soul presently incarnated on the planet Earth should worry about himself or herself and make sure that he/she is doing everything in his/her individual power to bring and hold the light on this planet, for in doing so he/she will assist with the Shift and will make it easier for those who do not initially transition. Are we making ourselves clear? This is an important message that we want you to get out to the people: stop judging others and instead put your considerable power and energy into pumping out positive energy.

I haven't actually heard anyone say aloud, "I wonder if she will make it through the Shift," but I often hear people use karma as a threat. "Karma will get you for that," or "You'll pay for that later." When we talk about karma that way, we are essentially using a Universal law as a threat! Bullying someone with Universal law is not a positive energy thing to do. When we do that, we are also making judgments about another person without having all the information. We don't know what Windows of Opportunity/Relationship Villains someone else has set up to learn lessons. For goodness sake, we are just learning to look for our own windows!

Gilbert and the Group are very clear here—judging others is wrong, and trying to establish who will transition during the Shift makes no sense. Souls are on their own paths of spiritual growth. Some group together for a karmic lesson, and some souls come together to work on projects, like the Shift. All of us have a purpose, and many who are incarnated at the present time are also here to help the planet heal and our species evolve. We are here to attract and hold the light and to pump positive energy into the atmosphere. Recognizing that we should spend our time taking care of our own business and not worrying about who transitions and who doesn't is a step towards expediting spiritual growth. By taking care of own business, we're also making it easier for our fellow entities that are on different paths. There are many paths to spiritual growth—there is no *best way,* only *the best way for me at the current time.*

Chapter Nine:

Will Animals Make The Shift?

It's no secret that I love animals. Throughout my life I've shared my home with many dogs, and now I find myself living with 13 wonderful cats that were all rescues. My husband, Ted, and I also feed tons of birds, raccoons, opossums, and whatever else shows up at our door—we've even see a fox eating cat food on our front steps! I donate a portion of the money I make from my jewelry and book sales to the Humane Society. One of the things that continues to weigh heavily on my mind and my heart is, "What will happen to all the animals during the Shift?"

Sherri, you are concerned about the fate of animals during the Shift, and we must tell you that there will be animals making the Shift along with human beings. Those animals that are able to adapt to the new energy frequencies will also evolve to the next level. Some species will evolve and some will not. Some dogs will evolve while others will not, and it will be so throughout the animal kingdom as individual animals, like individual humans, go or stay.

Animals are of a group soul—they gain independence and personality as they live their lives. This is especially true for those animals that live with humans—cats are simply cats, dogs are simply dogs, and ferrets are simply ferrets until they become part of a human family. Then they gain an identity and develop and evolve. Animals that do not interact with humans evolve as they are intended to evolve.

It is not always a bad thing when a species of animal becomes extinct. It certainly would be a different world today had the dinosaurs survived! When animals are threatened because of the conduct of human beings, that is a karmic debt that has to be paid. Sometimes evolution dictates that animals change just as human beings have changed and continue to change during their evolution. All are on an evolutionary path.

When the Shift is complete, there will be humans who evolve and there will be animal species that evolve and change with the planet. This is the plan that has been agreed on and will take place. Do not fear for those who do not Shift with the planet; it will be but a moment in time. Some will be back on the other side of the veil, and some will complete their current lives in the third-dimensional energy.

At this time, we would like to take this opportunity to say to you and to everyone reading this book that now is the time to pay great attention to what you are thinking, doing and saying, for these things will affect the transition for those who remain and those who go. We are in a time, dear girl, when our thoughts will become things much more quickly than in the past, and we are at a time when our words and our actions have meaning that is ten-fold what they have been before. This is a time of great acceleration, and the light is being brought to the planet in larger quantities than ever before.

This is an exciting time! It is also a scary time for many, and as you are so wont to say to people, Sherri, knowing doesn't make it any easier. Do not let fear interfere with your mission, and do not sit around all day worrying about your cats and the birds and the dogs and the raccoons and every other creature on the planet. If you want to make a difference for all citizens of the planet Earth, human beings and animals alike, then mind your 'P's and Q's' and pay attention to what you think, say, and do, for making those changes will help all have an easier transition.

I can't say that this is what I wanted to hear. I get the point about the dinosaurs, but I don't want one single creature to be afraid or to be harmed during the Shift. But wait; another thought just entered my head--maybe I'm not giving our animal friends enough credit. Maybe they are more awake than we are, and they know on a soul or group soul level what's going on with the planet? I'm also feeling that we can help our beloved pets raise their vibrations by sharing our light with them through petting them and by *intending* that their vibrations be raised. From this moment on, as I'm petting my cats, I'm going to focus on raising their vibrational levels and visualize them transitioning to the fifth dimension.

Chapter Ten:

Old Earth

Knowing that some human beings and some animals will **not** transition at the completion of the Shift, rational thought naturally leads one to the following question: what will happen to them and where will they go? Gilbert and the Group addressed these questions with the following dictation.

Ending the incarnation cycle is the ultimate goal of most souls who incarnate on planet Earth, and so we now speak about the souls who will remain here on what will be called 'Old Earth,' and those who will continue to incarnate at this third-dimensional frequency or energy.

There will be two planet Earths co-existing, the Old Earth and the New Earth. They will simply be vibrating at different frequency levels. Some will transition to the higher frequency; some will stay at the lower energy level. For those who have chosen not to transition, do not weep. All is as it should be. Souls have the option of staying or transitioning, and not every soul is ready, willing, or able to make the transition, and that is okay. There is nothing wrong with this, nor is this something for which others should sit in judgment.

Many religions speak about an upcoming 'rapture' and say that you may be walking down the street with a group of friends and suddenly find yourself alone as those around you suddenly disappear. There is a kernel of truth to this in that some will stay and some will transition, but it won't be that a 'rapture' has occurred. It will be the result of the completion of the Shift and the subsequent creation of a parallel planet resonating at a higher frequency.

Those who remain will deal with the things that will need to be dealt with here, and they will go on with their incarnations until they are ready to move on to a higher vibration. There are also entities that could certainly make the Shift but have elected to stay behind and continue their work on 'Old Earth.' Many Lightworkers will remain and rise to leadership positions and help the 'Old Earth' progress so that more of its inhabitants can raise their vibrational levels and eventually transition to the next level.

Remember, all is never what it seems, and that again is why we caution everyone to not judge other people. You never really know what their true mission is. They don't even know unless they are awake.

Will those who have elected to stay behind realize what has happened? The answer is both 'yes' and 'no.' Because they will remain in third-dimensional bodies and because they will still be part of the third-dimensional energy of this planet, for many, only their higher selves will know what is going on. The incarnated part of the entity will not know exactly what has taken place. However, there will also be those who do know what has taken place and will use that knowledge to help those on 'Old Earth' continue to evolve. Evolving into a fifth-dimensional being is the goal of all third-dimensional beings.

There is more about Old Earth and those who remain on Old Earth in Section Six.

Chapter Eleven:

Our Already Changing Lives

As I'm organizing Gilbert's dictation into book format, our economy is faltering. People are losing their jobs and their homes. There are scandals in the business world as companies pay CEO's huge amounts of money and continue to have expensive executive retreats and receive large bonuses after taking bailout money from the government. The banks are doing business differently and not lending money as freely as in the past, which may or may not be a good thing in the long run—I don't know. I do know that my company and a lot of other companies have been impacted by the banking changes, which have forced major layoffs affecting thousands and thousands of hard-working people. There is a trickle-down effect in action right now, and people are suffering more than any baby boomers have seen in their lifetimes. It's hard to be positive as we and those we love are losing jobs and homes. Gilbert has some insights about what's happening to share with us:

It seems dark now, but the changes that are taking place are happening for a reason. It's true that people are losing their jobs and people are losing their homes, but these things are Windows of Opportunity to learn and grow. In many cases people are finding work in other fields that will make them happier personally and will also allow them to contribute more to the overall growth of those around them—the people they touch on a daily basis. Many entities are currently experiencing situations that are life-changing, and while they seem overwhelming and terrible, these changes provide opportunities.

Sometimes they are opportunities to change paths and pursue the things they need to pursue for the good of their personal growth and for that of the planet.

One who loses a job but takes the opportunity to pursue a new career that is something that makes him/her happier or allows him/her to help other people is just one example of what we are talking about. Foundations are being shaken now. The people of Earth are being shaken to the core, but this is in accordance with the evolution that is taking place. It is true that much of what took place to damage the economy is directly related to actions taken by government and business within the United States, and again we remind you that the United States is Atlantis reborn. The Baby Boomer Atlanteans are struggling among themselves as they strive to make progress and overcome their group karma. Many tests have been passed now, and it is a time of waking up for this group, and this affects the world as a whole because of the sheer size of this group. Their actions affect the United States and the rest of the planet. Never before has such a large group incarnated together to work on or work out karma, so the effects of such an undertaking were not known in advance. The good news is that the group is firmly in the light and the current recession is something that was created by this group as a way to shake things up and wake up those who are still sleeping and on the wrong path. The current shake up is for the sake of spiritual progress, and while difficult to swallow and adjust to, eventually those affected will have that 'aha moment' and know that what they have endured helped wake them up or put them or kept them on the right path.

Again these changes are never easy but are necessary as we move toward the end of the Shift. Again, things

60

that seem catastrophic oftentimes have important reasons behind them. The recession is a tool for many to make changes that are important for them and for the world around them.

My husband lost his job after twenty years with his company, and he was devastated. Truth be told, I'm glad that he lost his job because it was killing him. He has now lost over twenty pounds, and his blood pressure and cholesterol are back under control. He just turned fifty-eight, but he looks like he's in his mid-forties, and no, I'm not just saying that because he's my husband! Ted hated going to work, and he complained about it every night when he got home. The money was great, but that job was causing trouble for Ted's health and for our relationship, too. I'm a person of action, and if I don't like something, I will make a change, so it was continually frustrating to me that he stayed in a job that he didn't like anymore. What kept him from leaving that job even though he KNEW he should? The money, for sure, and the fear of change, too. It felt *safer* to stay with a familiar situation even though he wasn't happy anymore, especially since it paid well. Losing that job was hard on Ted, and the loss of income was hard on our family budget, but it forced him to look for new directions. Eventually he started working on his own from home as an independent contractor for a similar company. He now sets his own hours, and he gets to be his own boss. Growing his business is slow-going during the recession, yet his sales increase a little every month. As the economy turns back around, the customer base he's worked so hard to establish will increase the size of their orders, and eventually, he'll have his money back, **plus** a job that he loves.

A year after Ted lost his job, I had to take three salary cuts: the first one was 20%, the second was 45%, and the third (and, I INTEND, the last one) was another 5%. This happened because the banking changes affected my company's ability to package and sell their mortgages. Over 6000 lost their jobs just at my company alone, and many resorts like the one I work

61

for closed down entirely. The day I got the news about the 45% cut in pay was the same day that my first book, *Windows of Opportunity*, came out. I may not be totally awake, but I have at least one eye open, and I can see that I'm being given a window to pursue other opportunities. The greatly reduced salary makes it very easy for me to open myself up to new things, and because of it, I started making and selling my own crystal and stone jewelry designs, and I started giving workshops about expediting spiritual growth. Angelic Channeler Jeannie Barnes (www.**angelicchanneler**.com) tells me that I will soon be able to leave my "day job" and I "intend" that she is right. Truly, though, without the nasty economic push that I received, my door (or window) would be locked to even the thought of making career changes, starting a jewelry business, teaching workshops, and pursuing writing full-time.

Several of my close friends didn't just take pay cuts, they eventually lost their jobs, too. And while things are tight and they've had to adjust their lifestyles big time, every single one of them looks better, feels better, and says they are happier. One now has twin careers as both a realtor and a photographer that give her the flexibility she's always wanted to spend more time with her son. It took another friend a little over a year to find the right job, but while she was searching, she found herself with some time to pursue writing and started writing a blog and articles that have developed quite a following. Another pursued her dream of having her own yoga studio, and it's the most beautiful studio I've ever seen. Another friend, who just lost her job a couple of months ago, is determined to carve out a new career doing something she loves and cares about this time around. Being part of very large company that downsized so greatly has opened windows for me to watch and learn from so many individuals who were overwhelmed by the loss of their jobs and are now rebounding and doing so in such a way that they are healthier and happier than they have been in years. Maybe Gilbert and the Group are right when they say that sometimes things have to be broken down and then rebuilt to get us back on our true paths. Speaking from *this* side of the veil, I think that is something that is much easier said from the other side, but then again, we *are* here to be on the front line of change.

> *It isn't really an economic decline; it is a time of great transformation as people become more aware of the things that are really important, namely entities in the guise of family, friends, and Relationship Villains, helping each other to achieve their goals for this particular lifetime. Preoccupation with huge houses and fancy cars is something that inhibits growth, and this preoccupation is going the way of the dinosaur as people learn to adjust their way of life and focus on the spiritual rather than the material.*

> *What is perceived as an economic downturn is actually a course correction that is a necessary part of the re-adjustment of the planet's energy. People are being forced to shed things and jobs that were sucking the positive energy out of them. Pursuing material things is not something that brings happiness or spiritual growth, and pursuing what has aptly been referred to as 'McMansions' is something that will make less and less sense to people as they continue to wake up.*

> *What is happening is part of the growth process even though it seems like the world is going backward. Sherri, this is such a hard thing to relay to you because you are so concerned with losing your job and your house, and so many are losing these things. But when a door closes, another door opens—that is the way with growth. For some, they cannot or will not make a change or move toward the light without a push or a nudge. You see the acceleration of such changes now because so many are choosing to make*

the move to a higher vibration, which brings with it the breaking down of existing paradigms in such a way that it appears the world is breaking down. It is not! Human beings are revamping themselves in the name of evolution.

I guess no one ever said evolving would be easy, and I think this section is a good reminder to take our power, face our fears (especially me), and move on with the mission of making this Shift as easy as possible for everyone.

Chapter Twelve:

Synchronicity:

Messages to Help Us Evolve

Just when I thought I was finished with this section, I began to feel like I was missing something important, but I didn't know what it was. Suddenly books, articles, and e-mails about synchronicity started to pop up every day, and it wasn't hard to figure out that the Universe was sending me a message. After reading James Redfield's books, starting with *The Celestine Prophecy*, I had put aside any belief in coincidences; however, I was still taken aback when a meteor-sized chunk of synchronicity struck me in September 2009 after I published my first article on www.Hubpages.com.

Readers can leave comments about their articles, and someone named Mary Soliel left a comment about mine. I felt a huge spiritual push to reply to her comment and in my reply, I told her I thought she should have a radio show. At the time I was considering doing a radio show of my own, and there was just something about Mary that screamed *great radio host* to me. It turned out that, unbeknownst to me, Mary had been experiencing synchronicities for months that made her feel certain she would somehow be on the radio, but she didn't know how it would happen. She acknowledged those messages and encouragement from Spirit and is now the host of *heaven Knows* on Blogtalk Radio.

But the synchronicity doesn't end there. Mary read *Windows of Opportunity* and wrote to tell me that there were a lot of shared references in my book and her book, *I Can See Clearly Now: How Synchronicity Illuminates Our Lives*. Mary sent me a copy of her book, and from the first page I was stunned by what I was reading because the content was so similar to *Windows*. We both quoted Kryon and Doreen Virtue, and many of the messages given to me by the GG for *Windows* were also included in Mary's book (particularly striking was the importance of our words and what we focus on)—simply in a different format. It was clear to both of us that we were caught up in a veritable web of synchronicity.

And there's more to this story! In January 2010, Mary invited me to be a guest on her radio show, and at the end of the hour, she asked me to share with her audience how we can work on raising our vibrations. I believe I said that the audience might think I was crazy, but the quickest and easiest thing that any of us could do to raise our vibrations and help the planet would be to smile. The day after that broadcast, I received an e-mail from Lightworker Jenny Oney, who is stationed in Reynoldsburg, Ohio. Jenny gave me her permission to share with you what she wrote:

> *Sherri, I had to share this with you. First, let me say that I have astounding synchronicities all the time, and I am on a mission to see what all of this means to me and my life. Well, last night before going to sleep, I listened to you speak on Mary Soliel's radio broadcast. At the end of your radio chat with Mary, you were talking about the importance of the simple act of smiling. I was thinking over all that you said while I decided I should get ready for bed. I took a few minutes to find the book that I am reading as I thought I'd read for a few minutes before falling asleep. As I was looking on my bedside stand for my book, my eye fell upon an object that I was unfamiliar with. Upon closer examination, I saw that this object was the size of a bookmark and had words written on it. I put on my reading glasses and the words read, 'Top Ten Good Things About Smiling' and then a list of those ten things followed. And when I turned the bookmark over,*

there were numerous yellow smiley faces all over! It was a smiley face bookmark! My mouth fell open! This synchronicity really 'packed a punch' as I encountered this bookmark only minutes after hearing you speak about the importance of a smile.

Every e-mail I receive is important to me, but this one really struck home, and here's why. Remember the radio show I talked about earlier in this book where the host asked me if I really thought smiling makes a difference? That took place a couple of months before I was on Mary's show, and that host asked her question about smiling on behalf of a listener who was chatting with her online during the broadcast (I've learned that it's common for chat rooms to be attached to radio broadcasts). Well, I trust in what the GG say to me, but when you say aloud, 'Smile, and it will help raise your vibrations and help the planet,' it does sound simplistic. That question made me second-guess myself a little bit, and I asked the GG if I had messed up on the dictation on this subject. They assured me I hadn't, and shortly afterwards I started seeing articles in newspapers and magazines about the power of smiling, and then I got that wonderful e-mail from Jenny! Synchronicity in action!

So what exactly is synchronicity, and other than the above making for a cute story, what does it have to do with raising our vibrations? First, let me go straight to a definition of synchronicity that Mary Soliel found in the May 2006 issue of *The Center for the New Age Newsletter* and included in her book, *I Can See Clearly Now: How Synchronicity Illuminates Our Lives.*

> *Synchronicities are people, places, or events that your soul attracts into your life to help you evolve or to place emphasis on something going on in your life. The more consciously aware you become of how your soul creates, the higher your frequency goes and the faster your soul manifests.*

Synchronicity is accelerating, begging for our attention...particularly since the dawning of the new millennium, as we are moving quickly toward great change and ultimately a more peaceful world...once you 'get it'—that you are receiving, actually attracting communications from the Universe...your whole life transforms into a magical, fascinating, and joyful journey.

And now I understand why the Universe wanted a section about synchronicity included in a book about raising our vibrations for the New Age. The higher our vibrational level or frequency, the easier it is for us to manifest the people and events that will help us complete our spiritual To Do Lists, which will help us evolve more rapidly. Do you see the similarities between a synchronistic event and a Window of Opportunity? It was no accident that I published on Hubpages and Mary commented on my article. It was no accident that I encouraged her to have a radio show or that I was later a guest on it talking about smiling. And it was no coincidence that Jenny Oney listened to what I had to say about smiling, and then found herself surrounded by smiles. One more synchronistic moment about smiles and we'll move on to some more words of wisdom from Gilbert and the Group. In 2008, I met a Lightworker named Viki Vertel, and we quickly found that we had a lot in common. Viki is a marketing professional and a very talented nurse, who decided to put her gifts to work by traveling to different countries with a medical team for Smile Network International. She helps give kids their smile, and I am always so happy when she has a few minutes to write or call and bring me up-to-speed on where she's been and what's she done. I also can't help the tears of joy that come to my eyes as she reminds me just how important a simple smile is to all of us.

Now let's hear more words of wisdom from Gilbert and the Group:

Be aware that there are Windows of Opportunity for you. As you watch for those windows, you will attract to yourself the communication you wish to receive from the Universe. Be awake and pay attention when someone you don't know starts talking to you or sends you a friend request on Facebook and pay attention when you start to see the same things over and over. Often there is a message to be heard, and you need to figure out what that message is. So many say that their angels or guides don't answer their calls, but, in fact, they do answer. Some will recognize the message even though they might not like the answer, and many do not pay attention to the answer—no matter how many times that answer is placed in front of them. We say to you that when the same number continues to occur in front of you, it has a meaning. When you hear the same song being played, it has a meaning. If you wake up with a certain song in your head, there is a message there for you that is important, and you need to think about what that message might be. Start by understanding that there are no coincidences. That will help you pay more attention to the small but powerful things that happen to you.

We would also say to you, Sherri, that as you become more skilled and competent at discerning the messages you receive daily from the universe, and all who are incarnated receive them daily, you will pay more and more attention to what is going on around you and spot those Windows of Opportunity. Raising your vibrational level is important but so is taking care of your To Do List for this incarnation. Synchronicity is a method of communication from your angels, your guides, and the universe. It would do everyone well to pay attention.

Whenever I start seeing the same numbers over and over again, I know there's a message waiting to be heard, and I run to my bookshelf for my copy of Doreen Virtue's *Angel Numbers*. Lately I've been seeing 444's. I wake up at 4:44 in the morning. I happen to look at the clock in my car, and it's 4:44—the number keeps on popping up, and when I read the meaning for it in Doreen's book, I found encouragement that I was on the right path.

This was an important message for me because I recently started doing workshops based on the material I receive from the Guide Groups, and I was wondering if workshops were the right course of action for me to take as a Lightworker. Adding to that message was a call from my friend Kathey Condon (Owner of Studio K Yoga in Kissimmee, FL), telling me about a yoga class she recently took at New World Wellness in downtown Kissimmee, Florida. She told me I should call the owner, Nicole Georgi-Costello, and talk to her about booking a workshop! How's that for synchronicity? Wait, there's more! I stopped in at New World Wellness a couple of days later and while chatting with Nicole and her husband, Craig Costello, Craig mentioned that the two of them had recently started drinking alkaline water. I nearly fell off the couch I was sitting on! I think I even slapped Craig's knee because I had just started drinking alkaline water three days earlier, and I was wondering if it was really better for you, or if it was just another scam.

A week earlier, I was with some friends that I mentioned in *Windows* (Heidi Winkler, Diane Diaz, and Grace Velez), and we were marveling over how much younger and how great Grace looked. She said a lot of people were asking her what she was doing and the only thing she could think of that she was doing differently was drinking some alkaline water that someone in her family had given her. She looked so good that I wanted to try the water, too. It turned out there was a store that sold it less than a mile from my house! As I watched the movie about the water and then bought some, I was thinking that anyone who knows me would say, "Geez, Sherri, you'll fall for anything you think will make you look younger!" Hey, you will, too, when you get to be my age! When Craig brought up the water, they both said how much better they were feeling from drinking it and that they were going to start carrying the water at their Studio. I knew that was a communication from the Universe that I wasn't being scammed. Being the frugal people that we are and having an aversion to paying for drinking water, Ted and I have decided to drink alkaline water for three months and see if it makes any difference for us. I'll keep you posted on the water, but do you see how I got my message from the Universe via synchronicity?

Gilbert mentioned that we should pay attention when someone we don't know speaks to us. On that note, let me share with you that I have met many wonderful and interesting people at workshops and conferences. Every person who has written to me or come up to me to talk after I've spoken at an event has given me something to think about. I'm a better person today because people I didn't know reached out to me, even if just with a few e-mails. So when Gilbert says to pay attention to people we don't know, that makes perfect sense to me.

One final thought as we end this chapter: the messages are coming. It's up to us to recognize and listen to them—another skill that we will master with practice.

SECTION THREE:

Our Atlantean Connection

Chapter Thirteen:

Why Are We So Intrigued by Atlantis?

On the subject of Atlantis, British historian H.G.Wells wrote, "There is magic in names, and the mightiest among these words of magic is Atlantis. It is as if this vision of a lost culture touches the most hidden thoughts of our soul."

And who isn't intrigued by the thought of Atlantis? I know I am!

Maybe we're so intrigued by Atlantis because *we remember it* on a soul level? Reincarnation makes it so that we are our own ancestors, and the Atlantean civilization is back in full force, trying to "Get it right" this time. *We* are trying to get it right this time.

Depending on what books you're reading, there were either two or three great periods of destruction in Atlantis. What they *all* agree on though is that Atlantis eventually did itself in *completely* because of their severe misuse of power and technology. They had weapons of mass destruction, they misused them, and they bullied other civilizations and races. Does any of this sound familiar?

We know that Atlantis eventually shrunk from a continent to a series of islands, and finally it was gone. Prior to the final destruction, though, there was enough warning for the people of Atlantis to exit, and according to Edgar Cayce, some went to Egypt, South America, even Arizona, and, listen to this—Cayce said that some went to the *Yucatan land of the Mayan experiences.* Is it possible that the very people who wrote the Shift prophecies were the displaced Atlanteans or their ancestors?

Anyone who watches the history channel knows that bits and pieces of what researchers believe to be the Atlantean civilization have been found in many different cultures across the planet. Of course, Plato wrote about Atlantis as an **advanced** civilization back in 360 B.C., which makes sense. The technology of the Atlanteans was no doubt developed to a point that was beyond the comprehension of mankind during Plato's time.

But **WHY** do **WE** think that the Atlanteans were so advanced? I'm sure our cars, planes, cell phones, TVs, microwaves, and DVRs would be beyond the comprehension of the aboriginal people of the Australian outback today. The perceived *advancement* of a civilization is very much a matter of perspective, and no doubt that the Atlanteans brought the human race to a higher technological level than had ever been previously achieved—especially from the perspective of ancient man.

And once you get started, it's easy to spot similarities between Atlantis and the United States of America, which we'll talk more about in the next chapter.

Chapter Fourteen:

Why Are the Atlanteans Here?

The Shift in Consciousness to the fifth dimension, the very evolution that we are struggling to complete right now, *could* have taken place during Atlantean times. It didn't happen then because, unfortunately, their level of spirituality didn't match their level of technology. They destroyed themselves and did great damage to other civilizations and to planet Earth. They were very close to taking human beings to the next level but, instead, ended up creating a huge amount of karma. And that's the point of *this* Atlantean experiment—the Atlanteans are back in full force:

- to do it again;
- to get it right; and
- to attain a level of spirituality that matches the current advanced level of technology, so that human beings can finally take the next step up the evolutionary ladder.

The significance of Atlantis with regard to our Shift is the fact that many of those presently incarnated and also lived in Atlantis and were responsible for the destruction of that continent. They are here now trying to work out their karma as a group. Because of their sheer numbers as they work through their group karma, they are in a position to have a tremendous effect on the vibrational level of our planet and, therefore, are very important to the human race as we strive to evolve to the next level.

In *Windows of Opportunity*, the GG wrote that much of our Baby Boomer generation is Atlantis reincarnated. Those

Atlanteans chose to reincarnate together at this time in history to work through their group karma, and they chose the United States as the location for a large number of them to incarnate. According to the GG, it is the largest group karma undertaking in the history of our planet, and they shared with us that George Bush and Al Gore were both Atlanteans on opposite sides of the political fence back then, as they are now. They also talked about the Bush/Gore election being a "temperature taking" to see how far this group had advanced in learning its lessons. During the writing of this book, Gilbert and the group made several mentions of Atlantis, which I've included below.

Oh, how we cringed when George Bush was elected president instead of Gore because that meant that you were not ready as a whole to move forward, and it was so close, so very close, to happening. And those next dark years and the re-election of Bush made us wonder if you could regroup as a civilization, but regroup you did. And Bush, well, he played his part well. Have you ever seen a better Relationship Villain for the time? He played the Villain and finally, finally, the United States, whose people are crucial to this experiment because the United States is the 'new' Atlantis—so many are reincarnated there from that time—woke up and got back on board with the election of Obama.

Is anyone feeling déjà vu? Many of us presently incarnated lived through the destruction of Atlantis, and we all know that Atlantis destroyed itself. And before they did themselves in, those in power bullied many of their own citizens at the same time they were at war with, and destroying, other civilizations. The desire for power and the misuse of technology by Atlantean leaders led to the downfall of what many think of as the most advanced civilization ever to have lived on this planet. The Atlanteans *were* advanced, and had they gone to the left instead of the right, their civilization would have been the first to facilitate the evolution of the human race to the fifth dimension. With the sinking of Atlantis and the destruction caused to the planet Earth at that time, the "great experiment" suffered an enormous set back. The "great experiment," the project that Atlanteans and others are here working on is this: to see if incarnated beings can evolve to a place in time where their combined vibrations will allow humanity to move to a higher consciousness.

All three of my Guide Groups agree that humanity has once again progressed to a place where such a transformation is not only possible and probable, **it's happening**. Two of the Guide Groups said that we were at a crossroads with the Bush/Gore Election, a "temperature taking" of sorts, to see how the group karma endeavor undertaken by the reincarnated Atlanteans was progressing. As I was doing some research for a lecture I gave at the 2010 Paranormal Explorations Transformation Conference where I spoke a little bit about our Atlantean connection, I found some information that that has led me to hypothesize that the Atlanteans reincarnated in large numbers here in the United States at least once before—during the mid-1800's. In writings about Atlantis by Edgar Cayce and Frank Alper, I found that while many Atlanteans were pro-slavery, a large faction of the population was anti-slavery. This faction rose up and caused a great political upheaval, a.k.a. Civil War within their culture. Take a look at what I found and see what you think.

- According **to Edgar Cayce's case readings in the book, *Edgar Cayce on Atlantis*,** the Atlanteans had a slave labor force. There was a faction of the population who didn't think this was right, and they wanted to make changes.

- In **Frank Alper's** three-book series, *Discovering Atlantis*, he also talks about a slave labor force referred to as "things," and he describes the types of work they were forced to do.

- Both Cayce and Alper indicate that slaves were bred in Atlantis, and in **Dolores Cannon's book, *Convoluted Universe, Book One*,** one of her hypnotherapy clients talks about "creatures" who were "termed of 'less pure' expression," mutations that were looked down upon by Atlantean society.

I don't think it's a coincidence that the issue of slavery was played out here in the United States 125 years ago, resulting in our own Civil War and the eventual outlawing of slavery after a five-year war that destroyed many of our own cities. I also don't think the city of Atlanta was named by coincidence, especially considering its role in the Civil War. And right about now, I'm wondering what parts Obama, Bush, and Gore played back then—could they have been Generals Lee and Grant, and maybe even President Lincoln? Is it possible that this particular time in our history was essentially a large group karmic learning experience for some former Atlanteans—a dress rehearsal of sorts for today's events?

Chapter Fifteen:

Making History

The Atlanteans that caused the destruction of their own civilization are back, and they are *us*! If you are a baby-boomer, you are very likely a reincarnated Atlantean who has a second chance to make history with this Shift. Never before has such a large group reincarnated together—and this group has chosen to come back now to right a wrong—to repay their karmic debt by helping humankind take the giant step that should have and could have been taken during the time of Atlantis.

Regarding Bush, Gore, and Obama, according to the GG they were all Atlanteans at the time of the great destruction, and then, like now, they were on opposite sides politically. In *Windows of Opportunity* and in the above passage from Gilbert, both guide groups have indicated that Bush is a Relationship Villain for this time in history. They noted that he has done a great job of calling attention to the negative effects of bullying and violence as a means of achieving peace, and that's what a Relationship Villain is all about, right?

> *With this election [of Obama], you have opened the door to great light shining down on this planet. And with that door open and with England, France and the rest of Europe already on board and Australia ready to go, you will begin to see the rest of the planet opening up to the light because, indeed, there are so many pockets of light in other countries and*

continents that it will not be long before the light is in the majority, and the Shift will be complete.

The GG believes that Obama will help the United States begin to heal relationships with other countries and continents. They also believe that he will help us start to think more globally, which is an important part of our evolution. We have to look at ourselves as being in this together with everyone else on the planet. We have to leave behind the old energy stuff like *"If you're not with us, you're against us."* Time will tell if Obama is the leader that both guide groups think he is, and at this writing, he has fallen a bit in the popularity poll. Seldom are great presidents thought to be great during their term/s in office—I'm pretty sure that Lincoln was not beloved by the South during his stint as president.

In the section above, Gilbert talks about Europe and Australia being ready to go, meaning that they are holding up their end of the project with regard to attracting and holding the light. That's why it's so important for the United States to get back on track as quickly as possible. We have to catch up with the rest of the Western world so that together we can continue to spread the light to those areas where it is needed. The Shift is a GLOBAL Shift. It is not a Shift of just one civilization like many believe happened with the Mayans. We are talking here about an entire planet and her inhabitants making the Shift to the fifth dimension. The following dictation about Atlantis is from Gilbert and Group, and because it was dictated on different days, it may seem a bit disjointed as you read it.

> *Sherri, today we will talk of Atlantis and the significance of this continent as it applies to the world today. Many Atlanteans are here now. Some have learned their lessons and want to be part of the solution, and others have not yet come around. This is an age that is indeed similar to Atlantean days. The technology and the types of energy used are different,*

but the mindsets of those in power are very similar to Atlantis. This is the challenge—the test of the Atleantean people to see if they can recreate Atlantis on Earth and to do it right this time.

Many who are currently incarnated are those who were originally incarnated in Atlantis at the time of the great destruction and who in fact played a large part in this destruction. We have told you before that this is a group karma endeavor. While this isn't the first time Atlanteans have reincarnated as a group to work out their karma, it is the first time it is being played out on such a large scale—this experiment of sending so many who were together before back to complete what they didn't complete the first time. And so it goes on that we are at a crossroads and which way will it go? The reincarnated Atlanteans have twice now elected a president who was only interested in the power and advancement of the United States, just as he was only interested in the power and advancement of Atlantis. Putting one nation or continent above all others is a selfishness that is tantamount to the fear that is being generated across the globe today.

It is sad that the Atlanteans were unable to change their ways at the first opportunity or even the second, but they are pulling together their energies and making progress.

Bush was prompted by others around him whom he saw as great councilors because of their experience in government and in business. It was hoped that Bush would recognize the bad advice and do things differently this time around. He had the power to overcome much karma and move things along, and we watched and hoped that he would do so. Still, although it took much time, Bush did help the United

States to realize that political bullying is not conducive to world peace. Enough Atlanteans are remembering subconsciously the old destruction and the old ways, and they are making a plea for a global outlook.

A global outlook is crucial at this point in the Earth's transition. It is one of the things that will help bring in more light and make the transition easier on all who are incarnated and on Earth herself. A global outlook is nothing more than allowing for the fact that all human beings have rights and the number one right is freewill. On this planet all revolves around freewill—it is the reason for incarnating here—to see if with freewill entities can remember their path and stay on their path. Freewill, coupled with the lower vibrations of the planet, make it challenging for human beings to stay on their planned path.

This is the great test, the great experiment. The good news is that more and more are choosing to take a global viewpoint rather than feeling that their country is the only one that counts.

So many wars have been fought on the basis of religion, but religion is not what inspired them. It was commerce, business, and wealth. Most of all, it is the desire for power that inspires wars and is the underlying factor of the stunted growth of the human race—the reason so many entities who are of advanced species have been brought to this planet at the present time.

As the journey towards the completion of the Shift continues, you will see a breakdown in the religious belief systems that are so important to the people at the present time. When people cease segregating themselves into religious groups that cause separation and start looking at humankind as a whole, great progress will be made on planet Earth.

We are not saying that people should not be spiritual. We are saying that people should be concerned about other *people, no matter what religion they might be. Yes, it is true that there are terrorist groups and terrorist cells, but as the United States stops being concerned only about the United States and fully wakes up to the knowledge that there are many cultures and ways of life that are just as important as the United States, then true progress will be made.*

You are concerned that we continue to speak of the United States rather than other parts of the globe, and we speak primarily of the United States because that is where the bulk of the Atlanteans have reincarnated. The United States is the new Atlantis. Because the actions and attitudes of these reborn Atlanteans is so important to the outcome of the great experiment, we tend to focus our attention here. All countries and cultures have their own karma and their own lessons for growth and advancement.

And now we wish to speak to you about something that is simply history, but we think your readers will find it interesting. In 'Windows of Opportunity,' the GG spoke about the Atlanteans and how they are reincarnated now as part of a group karma/re-development program, and that two chances went by [with the election and reelection of Bush] *for that group to make positive advancements and contributions AS A GROUP. Obama was eventually elected, and he is the proof that the group is making better decisions and opting for a peaceful way to grow and learn. Such decisions help them atone for the destruction they wrought when first together in Atlantis.*

The reincarnated Atlanteans are making progress very quickly now and taking care of a lot of karma. Karma that would have taken many, many lifetimes to atone for is being worked through during one lifetime. This is possible because they are doing it together as a group. By working together as a group, they are integral to the current evolution of the human species. A certain percentage of incarnated souls is required to resonate at a particular level for this Shift to complete. With so many Atlanteans here at the present time, if they did not make the advancement necessary in their thinking and actions, then this Shift would not be possible at this time. Now let us be clear—not all of the Atlanteans have stepped up. Some are still dredged in the old energy, but enough have stepped up to make this very big difference. Evolution can now take place.

We are the Atlanteans just as we are the reincarnated entities of many past civilizations. The purpose of incarnations is to move ourselves forward and wake up faster with each succeeding incarnation, so that we can eventually end the cycle of lifetimes and graduate to the next level. The next level for us is to become fifth-dimensional beings, and that's what we're working towards right now. All three Guide Groups indicated that we are going to take this evolutionary step, but how easy or difficult it will be for the planet, for those who transition, and for those who remain on Old Earth, is up to us.

SECTION FOUR:

2012

Chapter Sixteen:

We're Evolving, Not Ending

In Chapter Six, we talked about the importance of facing our fears. Fear is a powerful emotion, and fear of the Shift and 2012 has become a worldwide pastime. I am definitely not a *2012 Expert*, but I've attended lots of 2012 workshops, I've read everything I can get my hands on about it, and, of course, my Guide Groups have dictated a little bit about it, too. Based on my research and what's been given to me through automatic writing, here is my advice when it comes to 2012: (1) don't go to Vegas and bet the retirement fund; and (2) don't go on a shopping spree with your kids' college money either!

I have good reasons for this advice, starting with something that Gilbert dictated in January 2010:

> *Sherri, we know you are caught up in this 2012 hoopla, and we ask that you let everyone know that 2012 will come and go, but the Shift will end in its own time. It is the completion of the Shift we are talking about here as the planet is already experiencing changes. More changes will come. We know you will find this hard to understand, but this a very exciting time to be alive on planet Earth! This is an exciting time for the universe as representatives from many planets gather to watch history being made.*

> *We know you want more information on 2012, and all we can tell you is that 2012 is a date on the calendar.*

There is no way to know with certainty when the Shift will be complete. We can tell you that the human race has stepped up greatly in the last decades and because of that, things will not happen as was once predicted. Such is the power of every individual currently incarnated on the planet, and the vibrations of the planet and its inhabitants are about to undergo a great amplification in vibrational levels. The increases that will take place over the next three years will be greater than that of the last three decades combined.

Well. There's nothing like being taken to task by your Guides, but Gilbert is right. I *am* "caught up in all this 2012 hoopla." Do you know that there are 2012 countdown calendars online ticking down to the date second by second?

Thirty years ago, the Shift was something only the New Age/metaphysical communities were talking about. Now there's a disaster movie called "2012," documentaries on TV, and, believe it or not, there was even an article in Playboy magazine about 2012! The Shift has gone mainstream and its new name is "2012."

Frankly, I think it's hard to **NOT** get caught up in 2012, especially when you watch the news about the weather changes and the decline in our financial and economic systems. It's easy to visualize the Four Horseman of the Apocalypse (War, Famine, Death, and Pestilence) coming around the corner with an ETA of December 21, 2012.

So let's examine that 2012 date. I think we can all agree that the Mayan calendar ends on December 21, 2012. That's not in question. But **who** decided it would be the end of the world? Lee Carroll, who channels the entity Kryon, has been to the Mayan Ruins and has spent a lot of time investigating the 2012 predictions. In January 2009, Carroll published an article about 2012 called "The Doom Factory"

[You can find the article in its entirety at www.kryon.com/2012blog.html], and here are two points he brought up in the article—both of which made so much sense to me when I read them that I wanted to share them with you:

1. Nothing sells advertising space like the on-coming destruction of our planet. 2012 makes for great copy, great reading, and movie ticket sales. Most of us have known about the Shift for decades, but it's gone mainstream now precisely because we're getting closer to the date, and again, disaster sells. 2012 is a huge moneymaker. Scaring the pantyhose off of us sells newspapers, magazines, and commercial time on TV. People are getting rich from the IDEA of 2012 being the end of the world.

2. The Mayans, the Egyptians, the Hopi, the Aztecs, the Toltecs, the Druids, and the Incas have all predicted a Great Shift. None of them predicted the end of the world, but for some reason, possibly because the Mayan's ended their calendar on 12/21/2012, the Great Shift is now being interpreted as *the END*.

How and when this happened, I don't know, but I do know that Lee Carroll wasn't alone at the Mayan pyramids. He was with Jorge Baez, who wrote a book about 2012 (*The Vital Energy of Movement: The Secret of 2012—as of 3/31/11 it is available only in Spanish)*) and, more importantly, Baez can read and translate Mayan hieroglyphics. Together Carroll and Baez looked at the glyphs on the wall of a Mayan pyramid, and here's what they found.

- The Mayans **did not** write about the world coming to an end.

- They **did** write about a great Shift.

- They **did** write about energy cycles, and

- They **did** write that one of the highest vibrations that the Earth had ever seen would return and be amplified, and that would happen at the time of the galactic alignment, which they predicted for 2012.

I'm not a scientist or an astronomer, and you probably understand what the galactic alignment is better than I do—all I can say is thank goodness for the Internet so I can look this stuff up!

- The Galactic Alignment is the alignment of the December solstice sun with the Galactic equator—hence the December 21st date. Think Fall Equinox.

- The Galactic equator is the midpoint of the Milky Way Galaxy. Picture the Milky Way like a disk. The Galactic equator is the halfway point between the top and bottom of that disk.

- Something called the solstice point is the precise center-point of the body of the sun as viewed from Earth.

Now that we're all on the same page with regard to what the Galactic Alignment is, let's take another look at what the Mayans' glyph's said: a very high vibration would return and be amplified at the time of the galactic alignment, which they predicted for 2012. Nowhere on that pyramid wall did it say the world was going to end when those two things happened simultaneously.

And now comes the REALLY INTERESTING part of what Lee Carroll discovered. He says, and so do many others, that the **2012 alignment predicted by the Mayans was off by about 5.5 degrees, and it has already happened**! This is due to an error that the Mayans had in their calculations. Being off by just 5.5 degrees is pretty good considering the technology they had to work with back then!

Carroll and other 2012 researchers say that according to our scientists, working with today's technology, *"The precise alignment of the solstice point with the Galactic equator was calculated to have occurred in 1998."* We made it through! And this correlates to what Gilbert has said about us already being in the Shift and that it's the culmination of the Shift that we're all working towards. Again, exactly when that will take place is something that can't be predicted. What we do know, though, is that this Shift is a Shift in consciousness, which means that the human race is going up another rung on the evolutionary ladder. **It's a time for celebration, *not* fear.**

By the way, according to Lee Carroll, the Mayans made predictions that went beyond 2012! Clearly, they wouldn't do that if the world is due to end in 2012. Just why DID they end their calendar on December 21, 2012? Astronomer Phillip Plait has a theory about this that I'd like to present for your consideration. Plait says that the Mayan calendar is like a car odometer, and the December 21, 2012 date is the point where it would click over to a new cycle—kind of like an odometer clicks back to zeros after it reaches the 9s. I much prefer this odometer analogy to the interpretation that the end of the calendar means Apocalypse time. How about you?

And speaking of the Apocalypse, let's take a quick look at this word that is so often used in conjunction with 2012. The very mention of the word Apocalypse now strikes fear in our hearts, but what does it really mean? Surprisingly and perhaps fittingly, it means *revelation* or *the lifting of the veil*. That sounds a lot like evolution to me. I asked Gilbert for some insight, and he dictated that it means that we will finally be awake to who we really are, and what we are trying to accomplish. Think about that. We will finally, on THIS side of the veil, be awake and know what our goals are for our lifetime. We won't have to worry about spotting Windows of

Opportunity; we'll be able to learn our lessons and have our experiences without being asleep at the wheel.

Whether we call it the Shift, the Apocalypse, or 2012, the result will be the same: as our consciousness Shifts, we will leave an age of darkness (the veil is down/3rd dimension density) and move into an age of light (the veil is lifted/fifth dimension energy) and we will evolve.

I recently read *Phoenix Star, an Adventure of the Spirit* by author, healer, spiritual teacher, and radio host, Kiernan Antares. After appearing on her radio show, I asked Kiernan if she would share some of her insights about 2012 for this chapter, and she kindly agreed to share some thoughts with us:

> *The vision that flowed through me while writing 'Phoenix Star' was that of a cosmic moment in which Divine energies bathed the Earth, lighting up and activating all the dormant power points, vortexes, and sacred sites on the planet while at the same time downloading wisdom, knowledge, love, peace, and harmony into the hearts, minds, and souls of every individual who is willing and ready to graduate into a higher dimension. This cosmic birth heralds in a period of transition, a deepening of the cleansing and purification we are experiencing globally and individually, which will aid us in redefining our priorities with peace and unity consciousness as our guiding North Star. This will lead us into the Golden Age. As each one of us takes responsibility for our thoughts, feelings, and actions, and heals our wounds, surrendering to the power of love and the Divine Feminine energies at work, we will make this transition easier for the whole. There will be less planetary purification required, so it's important each of us does*

94

our part by cleaning our Home and turning on the Light.

Kiernan has such a wonderful way with words; I especially like her phrase, "...graduate to a higher dimension." We take on these different lives and personae in order to learn, grow, eventually finish our lessons, and graduate—and in this case, our graduation means becoming a fifth-dimensional human being.

Chapter Seventeen:

Is the Shift Ending on 12/21/12?

The GG talked about 2012 briefly in *Windows of Opportunity*, with some of what they spoke about originally given in 2004, and with additional information added in 2008. I'm guessing that many readers noticed the difference in the timeline discussed by the GG, and I would like to use that divergence to kick-start a new dialogue regarding this volatile subject. Here's what the GG said in *Windows*:

> **2004**: *"...The changes leading up to the culmination [of the Shift] on December 21, 2012, have been going on for a very long time...it is difficult to say exactly what changes will occur because we don't know what the vibrational level of the planet will be in 2012."*
>
> **2008**: *"...the date 2012 is not written in stone...when the planet is ready, it will complete the Shift."*

Did the GG *not* know what they were talking about in 2004? Why would the information change from a fixed date to uncertainty about when the Shift would take place? The answer is simple and very, very powerful. Human Beings have a great deal of influence with regard to the evolution of our species. We are very powerful beings. As we continue to make changes that allow more and more light to be drawn to the planet and as we continue to create positive energy, we are altering our vibrational levels and the overall vibrational frequency of our planet. These changes affect the timing and severity of the Shift, or more precisely, the completion of the Shift.

When the GG dictated the sections about 2012 for that first book, they weren't included in a chapter called The Destruction of our Planet. No! They were in the chapter called Evolution, and this is something that is important for us to recognize and understand—we are evolving. That's what the Shift is all about.

I've heard and read about the Shift and the destruction predicted to accompany it for as long as I can remember. In 1991, I was so scared by what I read that I started reading survival guides. I recall a time when my sister, Kathy Seeley, and I would try to figure out what state to move to. We weren't sure what would happen to her state of New York, but we were pretty sure that my beloved Florida would be underwater! I was convinced that I would have to live off the land, and I wanted to be prepared. For a person who considers the microwave oven to be one of the greatest inventions of all time, it's funny to look back to a time when I was searching for information about what nuts and berries were edible and available in different states and trying to figure out which states would make up the new East Coast. The thought of the Shift scared me, no doubt about it.

The information I was absorbing back then is old and outdated news today. Since I started reading about the Shift back in the 1980's, the information coming through has changed dramatically. For goodness sake, it changed within three pages in my own book! Reading survival guides just adds to the fear and negativity surrounding the Shift. What we have been doing and what we must continue to do on a larger scale is to find ways to raise our vibrations so we that can minimize the Earth changes that are part of the ongoing impact of the Shift. It is essential that we do this for those (many of whom will be Lightworkers) who will remain on Old Earth.

At this moment, it seems that there will be natural disasters associated with the Shift just as the changes in our global economy are part of the Shift. But the good news, no, the GREAT NEWS, is that more and more of us are waking up and realizing that we *can* help the planet (and ourselves!) go through this Shift with less upheaval, less drama, and less pain.

Windows of Opportunity open for us every day, and it's up to each one of us to make the choice to increase our output of positive energy. If you think about it, we're already seeing signs that banking and real estate are starting to turn around, and I think it's because we've focused our attention on these areas. We truly are catalysts for change, and if we put enough positive energy into health care reform, we can make more and better progress there, too.

Our combined focus and intention do make a difference, and they are necessary to facilitate an easier transition. Gilbert says that we have initiated a great deal of positive change in the last decade, and the positive energies we are generating are going to accelerate over the next three years. I study numerology in my spare time, and I don't think it's a coincidence that Gilbert said three years of acceleration. The number three is thought to be a number of great power—it's the number of change and balance. Change and balance—those words make sense when you think about the Shift as part of our evolutionary path—a Shift in consciousness for us and for our planet.

That representatives from all over the universe are here to watch as we complete this phase of our evolution makes sense when you consider that this is the first time in universal history that an entire planet and its population will undergo such a Shift at the same time. That's why Gilbert says that we should be excited to be here—we are at the heart of a universal phenomenon!

The Guide Groups indicate that we're already in the Shift, and I believe that. The timing of the END of the Shift (not the end of the world) has and will continue to change as human beings continue to increase their vibrational levels. Why? Because as we do this, we change the overall frequency of the planet, and sooner or later the combined vibrational level of the human race and vibrational level of the planet will converge at a pre-determined frequency. The Shift in consciousness will be complete. Human beings will once again be in balance with the planet. And so, for the present time, I guess I will continue to contribute to my 401K although some small part of me was hoping to be able to blow it all on a trip around the world.

Please don't think that I'm making light of the Shift, but it seems to me that knowing exactly when the Shift will take place is a little bit like knowing when all the unpleasant things we planned for ourselves are going to happen. There's a reason we don't remember what we've agreed to experience and the lessons we planned to learn. That reason is simple. We wouldn't be able to live our lives in a normal fashion because we would be pre-occupied with thinking about what's coming down the road. How could we sleep at night if we knew that we would be involved in a terrible car accident next month or next year, or that we might even be the cause of that car accident? It would be very difficult to live our daily lives like that, and there would be no *normalcy* for any of us if we had an actual Shift date.

SECTION FIVE:

Our Galactic Heritage

Chapter Eighteen:

ETs

When I wrote the ET section in *Windows of Opportunity*, I was not a happy camper. There I was, trying to put together a tool kit for spiritual growth, and the GG insisted that I include a narrative about how the mice I thought were under my bed (when I was little girl—not now!) were actually ET's who came to visit me on a regular basis to do some *cosmic therapy* because I didn't want to finish this incarnation. I wanted to go *home*. According to the GG, these ET's gave me the memory of little mice friends to cover what actually took place. Even as I sit here writing this section about ET's now, I am still hesitant to discuss this subject. Reincarnation and karma are fairly common beliefs today, and you can have a conversation about them at a dinner party without repercussions. But to say that you were visited by ET's when you were five years old, well, that's something else altogether. **That** is something that still raises eyebrows and lots of doubts about your sanity, unless…unless you happen to be talking to someone who had an ET experience. Then you're comparing notes.

So many of my own fears were shattered when *Windows* came out that I shouldn't have been surprised at the positive response to that very small ET section. I've had many, many e-mails from readers who've told me of similar experiences, including much to my surprise, my own sister,

Debbie Smith, whose perception of what they looked like is remarkably different from my own memory.

After reading about my ET escapades, Debbie shared with me that at the very same house in Sparkill, New York, where I had the mice thing going on, she was having her own visitations from what she calls the *pink monster in black boots* or PMIBB for short. She kept this to herself for over forty years because our mom convinced her they were just bad dreams, but Debbie never forgot her PIMBB just like I never forgot my mice! During one Saturday morning chat session online with both of my sisters, Debbie told us what she remembers about the PMIBB.

Debbie describes her visitor as having pink fur that was like icicles, not smooth like an animal's fur, and she would find herself standing at a spot that was at the edge of our yard where the woods attached to our yard. The PMIBB would speak telepathically with her at this spot as she stood there frozen, unable to move, and terrified (she was 4 years old when this started). At the time of this writing, she hasn't remembered much more about it, except that her PMIBB also wore a black derby hat! This is just me speaking here, but if Debbie found herself at the edge of the woods behind our house, she would have had to be brought there either telepathically by the PIMBB or escorted there. The bedroom we three sisters shared was on the second floor of the house, and I can't see any of us going outside in the dark, walking past the huge and very scary weeping willow tree in the back yard, and then heading toward the woods. I think some joint hypnotherapy is called for to see what more we can remember about the mice and PIMBB.

From what I've read online and in several books about alien visitations and abductions, it's not unusual for ET's to project the image of an animal into the mind of the person they are interacting with—I saw mice; my sister saw a PMIBB (thus proving which of us is more creative), and others have seen owls or other animals. Whitley Strieber, author of *Communion* and *Transformation,* and other UFO researchers often discuss owls in their writings, so who knows?! Maybe Debbie and I did actually have ET encounters back in the 60's. For me, the GG explained the mice camping out under my bed, and in thinking about those mice now, two things come to mind: (1) up until the time I was around 11 years old, I continually bugged my mother to let me have a white mouse as a pet; I even brought one home once or twice, much to her chagrin; (2) I now live with 13 cats! Consciously, I thought I was put in a bad position when cats started having kittens in our bushes and feral cats starting showing up, too. Ted and I "fixed" every cat that walked onto our property, and some of them decided to stay and live with us. As we fed them every day, we fell in love with them. Is it possible that when I was eleven, I missed my mice friends and tried to replace them by bringing home live mice as pets? And then later as an adult who was terrified by the thought of alien abductions after reading ten books in a row about them, did I subconsciously create an army of cats to keep the ETs/mice away? Or did I just grow up to be a "cat lady?" Maybe both!

Truly, too many people have had encounters to ignore that such things have happened to many of us in the past, and many of us are involved in ongoing contact with our guides, angels, and beings from other planets and other dimensions. And there it is, ladies and gentlemen, my transitional sentence to move us into the nitty gritty of this ET section. I have had a new ET experience, and this one, as my grandmother would say, is a real doozy. There, I've warned you, so let's move on to the next chapter where I will formally introduce you to Akhnanda and the Arcturians: the third Guide Group to contribute to the writing of this book.

Chapter Nineteen:

Akhnanda and the Arcturians

Akhnanda popped in for the first time on June 30, 2010, as I was sitting under a huge oak tree in my front yard meditating with my new moldavite crystal (see Section Seven for more on moldavite and other crystals and stones).

I didn't really need another piece of moldavite (or so I thought), but I was really feeling drawn to this particular piece at a booth at the 2010 Ozark Mountain Paranormal Transformation Conference. About two weeks after the Conference, I finally had some free time and starting working with the moldavite. When a stone calls to you the way this one called to me, there is always a reason, and I was excited to see what would happen during meditation. As I held it in my right hand and closed my eyes, I immediately felt an energy surge in my third eye (see Chapter Thirty One), and then throughout by body, and I got a strong tingling sensation in my right hand and arm. I knew something was happening. As I started to hear Akhnanda speaking to me, I reached for my pad and paper because I didn't want to miss a word. Here is how Akhnanda first introduced himself to me—and believe you me, this is a section of dictation I *really* wanted to leave out:

> *Sherri, it is I, Akhnanda. I have come to say that I will very much enjoy working with you and taking you to the next level. You are of a high vibration because you originate from the Arcturian star system as are many Starseeds currently on planet Earth. But there is more that you can do to move yourself and others to a higher vibration.*

We, the Arcturians, have been waiting for you for quite some time, and we are very pleased that you are opening to your heritage, so to speak. We are the Arcturians, and you are an Arcturian Starseed as are many, many entities currently incarnated on the planet Earth. And there are many, many other Starseeds from other planets, star systems, and dimensions, particularly the Pleiades, who are now part of the human culture on planet Earth. All have come to help humankind and the planet move to a new energy level, a new vibration, and we will start with some simple meditations.

And that was my first dictation from Akhnanda; thereafter, it was "Akhnanda and the Arcturians." It quickly became apparent that their preferred method of communicating with me was during meditation sessions rather than automatic writing, so after each session, I quickly made notes so I wouldn't forget what was said. From time to time, I would ask a question and grab a pen and paper so I could get the answer down word for word. Not using my computer to "receive" information is definitely new for me, and I find that I really have to center my attention and focus heavily on what's being said to make sure I get everything coming through.

They asked me to meditate with the moldavite for twenty minutes each day. Then they channeled information about raising vibrations and dictated two energy meditation exercises to help us expedite spiritual growth and connect to the fifth-dimensional light. These exercises are in Section Seven, and they will help those who are drawn to them to connect to the Great Central Sun and to the Arcturian energy, which is of the fifth dimension.

Akhnanda and the Arcturians indicate that these meditation exercises will help us expedite our spiritual growth by helping us raise our energy levels so that we are more awake to see and act on our Windows of Opportunity. They also said that working with our chakras during these meditations would help us raise our overall vibrational levels and help us tune in to our guides, angels, and Higher Selves, so that we can receive guidance and assistance as we complete the Shift. Over the course of several sessions it became clear that the Arcturians want to work with Starseeds and Lightworkers (and it seems that one can be both) to help them increase their vibrational levels and to assist them with their work healing the planet, as well.

They were adamant that working with them is not an exclusive club, and that they are here to help us make the transition to the fifth dimension. If you would like to work directly with the Arcturian energy (and many of you already are and just aren't aware of it), call on them to work with you. In my sessions with Akhnanda and the Arcturians, they indicated that we can call on them by simply saying, *"I wish to have an Arcturian master work with me."* A master will come to you and work with you through the use of Arcturian energy to raise your vibrational level. If at any time you are uncomfortable with the energy work, you can ask the Arcturian master to leave, and you can re-invite him/her back at any time.

My first encounter with the Arcturians was very powerful, and I'm glad I was sitting under a tree and not driving my car. When you first start working with the Arcturian energy and an Arcturian Master, maybe start out while you're sitting or lying down! As of this writing (July 25, 2010), I've been working with Akhnanda and the Arcturians for about four weeks. I find them to be supportive and insightful, and I feel a great peaceful energy when I work with them. I hope they stick around and work with me for a long time to come.

Chapter Twenty:

The Great Central Sun & Arcturian Energy

We all know that we need to "attract and hold the light," but what light are we attracting and holding? Our Sun is a source of 3rd dimensional light—we have plenty of that here already. The light we want to attract and hold is fifth-dimensional light, and that light comes from the Great Central Sun. According to Akhnanda and the Arcturians, the Great Central Sun is located at the center of our Milky Way Galaxy, and it is the spiritual center of our galaxy. The Great Central Sun is the source for fifth-dimensional energy and high-vibrational fifth-dimensional light for our galaxy.

It is the light/energy from the Great Central Sun that Lightworkers are attracting and holding for the express purpose of assisting the transition of human beings and Earth to the fifth dimension. Because the Arcturians are a fifth-dimensional species, they operate at a higher frequency (energy level) than we do. They are already fifth-dimensional beings, and they are here to add their higher frequency and energy to ours to help us make the transition.

Chapter Twenty-One:

Starseeds & Our Galactic Connection

Akhnanda also shared that a transition, such as the one we're going through, a.k.a., the evolution of our species, is something that has to take place from within our species, which is why we have Lightworkers/Starseeds incarnating on Earth. Lightworkers and Starseeds are entities that have had lives on fifth-dimension planets or dimensions; therefore, they are familiar with the fifth dimension energy/frequency. By lowering their frequency level to be compatible with the 3rd dimension energy, they incarnate, sometimes many times, on Earth as human beings in order to help the human race progress. Whether we are Lightworkers, Starseeds, Third-Dimensional Human Beings or Fifth-Dimensional beings, we all originate from the same place. We are all sparks from the Creator/God. We are each on our own evolutionary path, and when we incarnate on Earth, we are all human beings. Because Starseeds/Lightworkers have already reached a fifth-dimensional consciousness at some point in their evolution, they are able to lower their vibrational level and "work from within" to help us advance.

Doesn't this sound like someone found a loophole in Star Trek's Prime Directive of Non-Interference? If you can't interfere directly with a less developed civilization, then utilize incarnation/reincarnation as a method to assist that less developed civilization—it's brilliant! Through the process of reincarnation, our species now includes human beings who are pre-wired with the ability to connect to the energy/vibration/frequency necessary to help our civilization evolve and become fifth-dimensional beings, and that ability becomes stronger with each planetary influx of Star Children (think Indigos, Crystals, and Rainbows).

Let's talk a little bit about Starseeds. The comment by Akhnanda that I'm an Arcturian Starseed is one that makes me want to run back into my closet and lock the door. Even though I've been told about my Arcturian connection in writings with different guides and entities (starting with Olexeoporath in 1987) and I've heard it from psychics and channelers since my first teacher, Cyndi, first said it to me in 1985, my feeling is this: Honestly, who wants to stand up and shout to the world, "Hey, look at me! I'm a Starseed!"

While it seems that it's time for all Starseeds and Lightworkers to come out of our individual closets, let's be realistic here. Admitting to being a Starseed makes saying that you take dictation from Spirit sound downright reasonable, don't you agree? But I'm told by my Guide Groups that most, if not all of you, who are drawn to my writing already know in your hearts that you are a member of the Lightworker/Starseed Brigade. So while I initially cringed and said, "No way am I putting this Starseed stuff into this book," here it is. I've learned over the years that you can't win an argument with Spirit; plus, my good friend and Reiki Master, Shelly Wilson, threw my own words about facing our individual fears right back in my face as she pointed out that talking about my Starseed connection is a Window of Opportunity! A really *big* one, I might add!

So what exactly does the term Starseed mean? According to Akhnanda, Starseeds are human beings who have had lives on other planets or in other dimensions, and who are presently incarnated on the Earth to assist human beings and the planet with their evolutionary transformation and are connected to the greater Galactic Community. Hmmm. The Galactic Community. Maybe that's why I daydream about being Counselor Troi and flying around on the Starship

Enterprise! A Starseed is a human being with galactic and fifth-dimensional ties, and this is a perfect segue for a discussion of the galactic community and our ties to it.

My time meditating and working with Akhnanda and the Arcturians has led me to the conclusion that part of becoming a fifth-dimensional human being is understanding, recognizing, and accepting our galactic connections. Yes, raising our energy/vibrational level is important but so is remembering who we are and where we come from. So I asked Akhnanda and the Arcturians about Arcturus, and here's what they said:

> *Arcturus is a 5th dimensional planetary system, and it is not noticeable to the human eye although you and we can alter our vibrations and energy patterns to work with and see each other. Arcturus is very much a way station for souls on various journeys, and it is a place of great peace and harmony. The bodies of Arcturians are light bodies, and no one needs or requires sustenance in the form of food or drink; energy is drawn from the Central Sun for sustenance purposes. We do not reproduce as you do. There is no need for reproduction here as we are part of an energy that is dedicated to the Higher Self and the evolvement of the human race and other species.*

Let me stop here for just a moment. After receiving this, I went back to the first writings I did with Olexeoporath in 1988, and one of the first things he said to me was that *"Arcturus is a way station for souls on various legs of their journey."* I never asked what he meant by that because I was just starting out back then and didn't realize that I could stop the dictation and ask questions. But as I looked at those first writings with Olexeoporath, and I was wondering what a "way station" is all about, I felt very drawn to pull out my copy of *The Prism of Lyra* by Lyssa Royal

115

and Keith Priest. In the Glossary of Terms for this book, Arcturus is defined as *"a way station for nonphysical consciousness,"* and in the chapter called "The Gateway of Arcturus," I found the following:

> *Because the gateway of Arcturus connects dimensionally with Earth, all who incarnate on Earth must pass through the Arcturian realm before they reach the planet unless they consciously choose not to. This provides a healing for those about to be born and a strengthening of their choices and desires for the physical life about to occur. At death the human consciousness passes through the Arcturian realm. There they are nurtured and cared for until they awaken to their greater reality. In case of traumatic death, a great tenderness and healing is shared so that the soul about to awaken makes a smooth transition.*

Now that we know what a way station is and the role Arcturus plays in helping human beings adjust before and after an incarnation, let's get back to dictation from Akhnanda and the Arcturians:

> *We are, indeed, in the pattern of life that you so urgently yearn for and that is because you know that it exists and you long to return to it. But you and the rest of the Starseeds and Light Brigade are on a mission of peace and healing and a mission to help humankind evolve, and for that we send our love and assistance. We will help you adjust to a higher energy as we know that for Starseeds being back in the density of the Earth's energy is like trying to fit a size 12 foot into a size 8 shoe. Earth is a difficult place to be when you have downgraded from a fifth-dimensional energy to a third-dimensional energy in*

order to do the work. The Arcturians and the Pleiadians are working with Starseeds/Lightworkers now to help you overcome your fear and the heartache that comes with being in a third dimension modality. That is why we are working with you now, Sherri, and why we wish for others to open up to our energy, so that we can assist Starseeds and Lightworkers to reconnect to fifth-dimensional energy.

Above, Akhnanda and the Arcturians mention the Pleiadians as another race of ETs who are here to assist us in our evolution. My Guide Groups have each dictated that there are two main fifth-dimensional ET species that are currently working with us and utilizing the connection that exists with Starseeds and Lightworkers to help us help ourselves evolve—they are Arcturians and Pleiadians.

We now know a little bit about the Arcturians, but who are the Pleiadians? I've read a lot of books with channeled information about the Pleiadians, and my favorites are both written by Amora Quan Yi: *Pleiadian Perspectives on Human Evolution* and *The Pleiadian Workbook.* According to Quan Yin, the Pleiadians are "Emissaries of Light," who, as "guardians of our planet," come periodically *"...to awaken us to where we are in our evolution and to what is needed in order to take the next steps."* I could quote paragraph after paragraph from these two books, but you get the gist of who they are—fifth-dimensional beings here to help us evolve.

Chapter Twenty-Two:

Our Galactic Heritage

At this moment I feel pressed to say that we need to work on our global heritage before we can truly progress to our galactic heritage. However, this is the perfect spot to explore our galactic *heritage*, so let's ask ourselves this question: Is it possible that we are not only being helped by fifth-dimensional beings but that we are *related* to them, too?

My first introduction to anything remotely connected to human beings as descendents of beings from other planets came during a workshop I attended in Tampa, Florida, sometime around 1993/94. The workshop was given by Lissa Royal, co-author of *The Prism of Lyra*, a book I mentioned earlier. In her book, Lissa contends that the Earth was seeded by extraterrestrials. She also states the following information:

1. The Pleiades is Earth's main genetic connection;
2. Arcturus is the archetype or future self-ideal of Earth and assists Earth in healing personal and planetary consciousness; and
3. A latent DNA code was placed within early humans and when human beings reach a certain vibratory frequency as a race, this DNA code will be triggered and will assist those on Earth in remembering their galactic past.

Admittedly, I do buy into the theory that the Earth was seeded by ET's, and I also buy into the theory that they have been working with us, seen or unseen, since that first seeding took place. I'm also of the mind that WE ARE starting to wake up to our galactic heritage, and here's one reason why I believe this is happening: when enough people put their focus on a particular subject and start to think and talk about it, then that subject matter starts to take a front seat in our collective consciousness. How do we know when this is happening? I think it's when the History Channel or the Discovery Channel do a series on a particular subject. In my mind that is a prime indicator that a particular subject is now at the forefront of our consciousness.

In April 2010, the history channel presented a four-part, eight-hour documentary called, "Ancient Aliens," the purpose of which was to provide evidence that we were seeded by and have had continual interaction with beings from space throughout our recorded history. Now you know that I wouldn't miss that series no matter what, but I *was* surprised to see several scientists providing feedback that buys into the galactic ancestry theory. Here are just a few of the highlights, all of which I think are worthy of our further thought, evaluation, and investigation:

- The statement that when we landed on the moon in 1969, we were technically the alien race visiting another world. And we were! Why do we think that we are the only race/planet that wants to or is exploring the galaxy?

- Excerpts from the Bible that could well have been descriptions/evidence of visitors from other planets and their spacecraft, for instance:

  o Erich von Daniken, author of *Chariots of the Gods* talked about how Moses had to go through a gate for his meeting with God;
  o The book of Ezekiel talks about visitations from heavenly beings coming down from the sky aboard heavenly flying machines; and

- o The book of Enoch talks about "watchers" that God put in place to watch over the Earth, some of whom "married the daughters of men."

- The various cave paintings/ sculptures/buildings/ writings from all over the world serve as descriptions/evidence of visitors from other planets and their spacecraft.

- Model airplanes found in 1898 in a tomb at Saqquara, Egypt, that were dated as having been created near 200 BCE. Similar airplane sculptures were found in Columbia.

- Cave drawings/hieroglyphics depicting modern astronauts found in caves in Italy, Utah, Australia, South America, and Mexico. One drawing in Mexico even shows a modern-looking breathing apparatus.

- Writings in different cultures about flying machines, including the Vimanas of Egypt and India. Again, think about what Ezekiel describes in the Bible.

- The Great Pyramid of Giza was supposedly constructed in 22 years by human beings alone. The solid blocks of stone used to build it weigh hundreds of tons. Architects say that even with today's technology, there is no way we could cut and move these huge blocks of stone and build that pyramid in 22 years. In 1877, it was discovered that this pyramid is built on the intersection of the longest lines of latitude and longitude on Earth, which puts it at the exact center of all the land mass in the world—its four sides even coincide almost precisely with the four compass points even though compasses were not known to have existed at the time the pyramid was built.

- Puma Punku, a megalithic ruin at Tiahuanaco, in South America, that makes the Great Pyramid of Giza look like small potatoes, is at least 14,000 years old, which means it dates to the Stone Age. Each stone is 200-450 tons, and they are made of Diorit, which is a material that can only be cut with diamonds. Exact cuts were made on the stones one centimeter deep and not one millimeter off from edge to edge. They were assembled like Legos to build a megalith that dwarfs the Great Pyramid of Giza.

- The Nazca Lines in Peru, when seen from the sky, look like airplane landing strips. This is also where from the sky you can see drawings of animals etched into the ground, and these drawings and lines date back to 200 BC. According to Giorgio A. Tsoukalos, Publisher of *Legendary Times Magazine* and who appeared on the History channel's documentary, Nazca may have been chosen "because it is one of the most abundant areas in the world regarding raw materials…it is the Cliff Notes of what we [meaning the planet Earth] consist of…"

As more and more people are talking about what they've discovered across the globe and as the Internet allows us to make connections between discoveries more easily and quickly than ever before, it's becoming increasingly more difficult to deny that we have a galactic connection. As we Shift to a fifth-dimensional energy and consciousness, we're not only awakening to who we really are, but we're also going to take our place among the galactic community, as indicated by Gilbert and the group in the following dictation:

"The new Earth will be host to many from other dimensions and other planets who wish to speak first hand with those who made this very difficult transition from a planet of duality and karmic influences to a planet of light. The first inhabitants will serve as a beacon of light in the universe—they will be living proof that this can be done, that great adversity can be overcome, and that souls can learn and grow in the midst of the most difficult and challenging of situations."

What Gilbert dictated above coincides with much of the information being channeled now and in the past about ETs watching to see how this all plays out. Acclimating to the possibility that we have galactic ancestors is something that comes with our growth and progress as we evolve.

It's as if "Evolution" is the name of a hot new Broadway play starring the human race, and the Galactic community is cueing up for front row seats. The good news is that we are not going to disappoint! Our reviews will be *stellar* (sorry, couldn't resist that pun). We will Shift, and then we'll take our place in the Galactic community and lend a helping hand to others while continuing to evolve. What, did you think this Shift was the end of our evolution?

SECTION Six:

The Transition

Chapter Twenty-Three:

We're Evolving!

If it takes a whole village to raise a child, how many souls does it take to help the Earth Shift to the Fifth Dimension? This unparalleled and celebrated time in human history wouldn't be happening without the hard work of everyone involved in this mission—past, present, and future! Our individual and collective contributions towards raising the frequency of the human race and the Planet Earth are paying off. Even through the challenges of the Shift, many of us are awake enough to see that progress is being made daily. Here's a little bit from Gilbert and the Group about our evolution:

There are those who will scoff at the information now coming through from many channels to your side of the veil, but the fact of the matter is that evolution is taking place. We've spoken about evolution in the past and when we did, we did not realize how close at hand the next stage in human evolution would be. That is how quickly things are changing!

Sherri, the great experiment to see if souls could incarnate in a world of duality and hardship and still find their way back to the Source is a success. The reward, the culmination of this great experiment, is the evolution of human beings to a higher energy, a higher level of existence, one that has never been achieved before by humankind on the Planet Earth. And because the planet will evolve at the same time, this is a sensation for the universe and something that all entities involved in the mission should be proud of. This evolution will see the Earth's inhabitants taking their place among the rest of the universe as a galactically awake and contributing race of entities, instead of a race of people with amnesia who are struggling to break free of third-dimensional energy and karmic ties.

Gilbert and the Group continued their discussion about our transition a few days later with the following information:

The bonds and shackles that are part of the fear-driven, karma-driven third-dimensional lives on Earth will be removed. Those who transition will have trouble adjusting to all of this in the beginning, and there will be a period, not unlike the Renaissance, where those incarnated will go through the motions of leaving a dark age and entering the light. Eventually all will come to terms with becoming fifth-dimensional beings.

I never really thought about fear and karma as being bonds and shackles and didn't really pay a lot of attention to this analogy by Gilbert until Lightworker Shelly Wilson shared with me something that happened to her when she was having some energy work done recently. Shelly told me that she could feel her legs move and lift up, and the person working on her told her that she had shackles around her ankles that were now removed. As I'm thinking about it now, I see that karma is about bonds and shackles in a way because we are bound to other entities and to lessons that we need to learn. Once we learn the lesson, the shackles of that lesson are released, and I think it's probably the same with fear.

Just take a moment, sit back, close your eyes, and imagine how great it will be when we don't have to deal with fear anymore! It will be amazing to know who we actually are and to take our place among the other fifth-dimensional races. It makes sense that those who transition will find themselves a little bit disoriented as the human race adjusts to the higher energy/frequency. I liked Gilbert's reference to the Renaissance, so I did a little research on our most recent Renaissance. It started in Italy around 1350, extended to Northern Europe around 1480, and ended sometime around 1700. That means the Renaissance lasted for approximately 350 years—that's a long time here on third-dimension Earth! Historians define this period as one that affected the lives of millions and changed the way people thought—sounds a little bit like our current Shift in Consciousness, doesn't it?

Chapter Twenty-Four:

Parallel Universes

Those who transition and those who will eventually incarnate on New Earth will be involved in great pursuits that will help other planets make the same transition that the Earth will soon complete. You see, this is the first time that an entire planet will be making such a transition. Entities transition, and that has taken place in many places and on other planets many times throughout the course of history; however, for an entire species to Shift at the same time as the planet, no, it has not happened before.

Have other groups of people on our planet made this kind of transition? I know that I have read many times, and you probably have, too, that the Mayans didn't disappear—many believe that they transitioned to a higher frequency level. I've also read about American Indian tribes that disappeared—the Anasazi come to mind—and some believe that they also transitioned. During my research I also came upon this little nugget more than once: there is a school of thought that the Mayans were descended from the Lemurians[1], and the American Indians were descended from Atlanteans. It's intriguing to me to contemplate the idea that some of the descendants of past races (who came close to the evolution

---

[1] Lemuria was an ancient civilization which existed prior to and during the time of Atlantis. Physically, it is believed that Lemuria existed largely in the Southern Pacific between North America and Asia/Australia. Like the Atlanteans, the Lemurian people were highly evolved.

we're in the middle of) might have actually transitioned to the next level.

When I logged onto the Internet to do more research, I discovered that there's actually quite a lot out there about these groups and others transitioning to a higher dimension. On the other side of the coin, I also found articles that said these groups didn't simply disappear; they disbanded or left their cities for reasons of political upheaval or floods, etc. Which is true? I don't know, but it seems to me that it is entirely possible that small groups of connected entities could raise their collective vibrational level to a point where they could transition. But where would they go if the New Earth is the result of the Shift that we haven't completed yet? Will those who transition to New Earth include the ancient Mayans? According to Gilbert, when such a group ascends, they vibrate at a level that is different from our own, and they can occupy the same space. That would mean that the Mayans are still here with us. We just can't see them—and that sounds like a reference to a parallel universe.

So let's talk parallel universes, a.k.a., the multiverse. This is the stuff of science fiction, not *real* science, right? Yet you can't read about or research parallel universes without also learning about quantum physics, and quantum physics *is* a *real* science, right? I found the following excerpt about Hugh Everett's Many Worlds Theory in an article titled **"Do Parallel Universes Really Exist"** by Josh Clark (you can read this article in its entirety at http://science.howstuffworks.com/ parallel-universe1.htm):

> *In 1954, a young Princeton University doctoral candidate named Hugh Everett III came up with a radical idea that there exist parallel universes exactly like our universe. These universes are all related to ours; indeed, they branch off from ours, and our universe is branched off of others. Within these parallel universes, our wars have had different*

outcomes than the ones we know. Species that are extinct in our universe have evolved and adapted in others. In other universes, we humans may have become extinct. This thought boggles the mind, and yet it is still comprehensible. Notions of parallel universes or dimensions that resemble our own have appeared in works of science fiction and have been used as explanations for metaphysics. But why would a young up and coming physicist possibly risk his future career by posing a theory about parallel universes? With his Many Worlds [or multiverse] theory, Everett was attempting to answer a rather sticky question related to quantum physics: why does quantum matter behave erratically?

What a noteworthy choice of subject matter for this experiment—using the theory of parallel worlds to answer a question about quantum matter. We can see why his future scientific career was threatened by the postulation of such a thought. Mr. Clark's article goes on to say that while we can't be aware of our other selves as a way to prove that there are parallel universes, there was an *imagined experiment* called Quantum Suicide that took place in the 1990's, the objective of which was to prove or disprove Everett's Many Worlds Theory.

An *imagined experiment* or a *thought experiment* is basically a proposal for an experiment that tests a hypothesis or theory. Because it might not be possible to actually perform the experiment in question, the goal of an imagined or thought experiment is to explore the consequences of the experiment if it were possible to carry it out. Thought experiments are not at all uncommon in science and are likely to be precursors to physical experiments (if it's possible to perform them). Imagined experiments have been performed by many of our great scientific minds, including Einstein (Specialty Theory of Relativity), Galileo (Principle of Relativity), and many more.

Sometimes these thought experiments are able to be proven by other empirical means, that is, from experience or observation without reliance on theory.

Let's get back to the Quantum Suicide imagined experiment that was carried out to try to prove or disprove Everett's Many Worlds Theory. An imagined experiment is carried out hypothetically, but it's based on data observed in quantum physics. You can read about the Quantum Suicide experiment in a second article by Mr. Clark, which can be found at http://science.howstuffworks.com/quantum-suicide3.htm. This experiment, as far as I can tell, did not disprove Everett's theory.

Clark includes in his article the following quote from noted Danish physicist, Neils Bohr, who won the Nobel Prize for Physics in 1922: "Anyone who is not shocked by quantum theory has not understood it." What exactly is quantum theory? It's hard to put into a few sentences, I can tell you that! Here's a very short definition that hopefully will suit the purpose of our discussion. It's a theory in physics that studies the basic building blocks of all things based on the principle that matter and energy have the properties of both particles and waves. It provides a mathematical description for the behavior of particles and waves at atomic and subatomic levels and is used by physicists to explain a wide range of physical phenomena relating to energy and matter; i.e., atomic theory back in the 1920's.

I can't say that I totally understand quantum theory. Everything quantum is a little bit on the mind-boggling side to me even though I strive to understand it. Going back to Bohr's comment, what's shocking about quantum theory to me is that the more I read about it, the more it appears that the accepted science of quantum physics is actually playing *catch up* (as Heidi Winkler would say) to metaphysics. Metaphysics is an ancient Greek word, with the prefix "meta" meaning "over and beyond." So the word metaphysics means "over and beyond physics." So those of us who study metaphysical subjects, like meditation, reincarnation, yoga, and ESP, could conceivably be considered "meta-scientists!" I'm joking, of course, but it does seem like the lines that science has drawn are being erased. When we transition to the fifth dimension, I'll bet we find that science and spirituality are both important components of the truth as we discover who we are and where we came from. Here are two examples of where the lines have already faded:

- Everett's Many Worlds Theory undermines the concept of linear time, and isn't that something we've been hearing and reading about through channeled information for decades—that time is NOT linear?

- The Many Worlds Theory also allows for us to have *other selves*. For decades we have been receiving channeled information that we are aspects of our Higher Selves and that sometimes there are many aspects of our Higher Selves walking around Earth (or even other planets and in other dimensions) at the same time.

Isn't it nice to know that the things we've known on a soul level are being theorized and hypothesized about by university students and scientists?

Chapter Twenty-Five:

Choosing to Stay on Old Earth

Sherri, we are here and ready to get started. Let us turn our concentration to how one arrives on New Earth. Some will transition there, meaning they will evolve from a third-dimensional human to a fifth-dimensional being and find themselves on a planet similar to yet different from Old Earth. In the beginning, reproduction will exist as it currently does although it will be much less painful. Therefore, entities will be born on the New Earth to those who transition. Because the New Earth will be part of the galactic family, there will be entities that visit and relocate there from other planets.

Let us speak of the transitioners, as that is the point of this book—to assist in the transition. To transition to the New Earth, one must have compatible vibrations with the new planet, meaning that one must raise one's vibrations to a fifth-dimensional energy in order to make the transition. Some are already at that level of vibration, some are close, and others are choosing not to go while some continue to require a third-dimensional density or modality for their growth.

The planet Earth as it is now is one of the most difficult places to learn and grow. Why? Because when entities incarnate here, they have no 'Earthly' idea who they really are, and the 'why' they are here is a journey filled with challenges. Third-dimensional Earth is a place where entities must start from scratch

137

each and every time, and the expectation and anticipation is that we find our way and progress more rapidly each time as we endeavor to wake up and remember our lessons and spot our Windows of Opportunity.

Incarnations of this nature will continue on the Old Earth for those who choose to remain behind and continue their growth this way. Not all will make the Shift at this time. This is as it should be, as many require the third-dimensional energy of the Old Earth to learn and grow. These entities will evolve when the time is right for them to evolve.

The Old Earth? "Those who choose to remain behind?" According to Gilbert, the planet will continue to exist in this dimension, which the Group refers to as Old Earth. I thought those who didn't transition would head back home to the other side of the veil and plan their next incarnation. According to Gilbert and the Group, many souls will do just that while others who are currently on the other side will continue with incarnations on Old Earth. Old Earth will continue for those souls who still have more work to do involving karma and life lessons, and third-dimensional Earth has the correct density/duality (separation of body and spirit) for this type of learning. According to Gilbert and the Group, New Earth will exist in the fifth dimension at the same time as Old Earth continues at its current third-dimensional vibration.

How is such a thing possible? I thought this information was so *out there* and confusing that once again, I considered leaving dictation out of this book. And then two things happened to change my mind:

- Within days of my thought to leave out references to Old Earth and save them for a future book, my friend, Heidi Winkler, told me over lunch that she was very excited about a book she was reading about parallel universes. She read that each time we make a choice, we live that choice, but a different universe is created where we make the other choice. If true, there are an infinite number of universes where different versions of ourselves live lives based on the consequences of each choice we make. This means there is an infinite number of planet Earths already in existence, so how far-fetched is it to have one more?

- Within days of this conversation with Heidi, I found myself waiting in my car while my niece, Lauren Ihburg, was running into the store, and I noticed my copy of one of Dolores Cannon's *Convoluted Universe* books sitting between the seats. I picked it up, and it opened right up to a page that showed a diagram of the New Earth splitting away from the Old Earth! I've had this kind of thing happen to me before when I've thought something was too out there to include, so I knew right away these things were no coincidence. I was experiencing synchronicity, and the message was loud and clear to leave in the dictation that mentions Old Earth.

Chapter Twenty-Six:

The Other Side

The following material was dictated after I asked my original Guide Group (the GG) on the Windows of Opportunity project: "If human beings are third-dimensional and we're evolving to the fifth dimension, what happened to the fourth dimension? Why are we skipping it?" You probably already know the answer to this question, but until they answered my query, it never occurred to me that what we refer to as "the other side" or the "other side of the veil" is, in essence, the fourth dimension. We are fourth dimensional beings when we are on the other side, which means that we have all had lots of experience transitioning between dimensions!

Sherri, when we cross over to the other side, we are greeted by those we knew and loved when they were incarnated with us during our most recent and previous lifetimes, and we are also welcomed home by our guides who, although unseen, were with us for the entire incarnation. Rounding out the welcoming committee are whatever teachers and friends happen to currently be on the other side at the time of our arrival.

The initial welcome is followed by a big homecoming celebration, which is then followed by a life review. This review is not meant to make us feel badly about things we've done or wish we hadn't done or even things we wish we did but didn't. It is all about measuring our learning and growth and the fulfillment of our debts and goals.

What we need to remember is that when we are in body we don't know "what is what" because of the veil. For that reason, something that seems like it was bad or mean might have been the right thing for growth when you look at it in relation to the grander scheme of things for that incarnation. It may be that by doing something that appears on the surface to be unkind, you were acting as a Relationship Villain or fulfilling a contractual obligation to another entity. And so my point here, Sherri, is that the life review is necessary but not for the purpose of punishing us for supposed 'sins.' The life review affords us the opportunity to understand all the nuances of what we experienced while in body and see how those experiences helped us with our intended goals.

For those who wish a five star life review, we direct you to pay attention to life scripts. Recognize patterns of behavior that are repeating in order for lessons to be learned and alter your behavior to stop the pattern from continuing to repeat. In other words, learn the lesson close to the ground floor.

This information is consistent with material from the GG that appeared in Windows of Opportunity. This is another reminder for all of us that it is we who are ultimately in control of our spiritual growth. We may have guides and counselors and friends to give us advice and help us formulate our life plans, but at the end of each incarnation, who is it that we answer to? Ourselves. While we may not initially be able to discern if an action we've taken (or someone else has taken) is consistent with our spiritual To Do List, there is one thing we *can* be sure of: if the same type of situation continues to occur in our lives, then we have a life script and a Window of

Opportunity that is calling to us, hoping to be noticed. So be aware of what's going on in your life and if you recognize something familiar in a situation, see if you can connect it to a similar situation in your past. If yes, analyze how you handled it in the past, and change your behavior accordingly. That's how the GG say we will learn our lessons faster and with less drama and pain.

The following material is from Gilbert and the Group. This dictation was part of a series of sessions dealing with how powerful our thoughts and words are. I was surprised to learn that philosophies and beliefs can be so strongly ingrained in our psyches that we could conceivably carry them over as we transition to the other side.

Let us now discuss the difference between what is perceived as heaven and compare it to fifth-dimensional Earth because there are elements of the New Earth that may be considered 'heaven-like.' Regarding heaven, there is no such thing as heaven and there is no such thing as hell, except for what one creates in one's own mind. If people are ultra-religious and feel like they will go to heaven for all the good things they have done and if that's what they are truly expecting when they cross over, then they will find their version of heaven waiting for them. It is the same regarding hell. If that is what people expect, then that is the immediate experience they will create for themselves.

When entities create a version of hell for themselves, their guides and loved ones quickly get to work to rescue them and help them remember who they are and where they are. When an entity creates this type of homecoming, it is certainly unpleasant; rarely a James Joycean type of thing—but a hell of his/her own making nonetheless. How does this happen? We are very powerful, and we are all sparks of the

Creator. What the Creator can do, to a great extent we can do as well. We can temporarily create this type of a reality for ourselves if such a concept has been entrenched or deeply rooted in our psyche.

Once you cross over to the other side, it will be YOU who will judge how well you have done, and that will take place, of course, when you do your life review. There will be no judge and jury making rulings and issuing statements about what you accomplished or didn't accomplish—you are your own judge and jury. You will take the lessons you've learned and apply them during future incarnations so that you can progress more quickly the next time around.

I believe in reincarnation and karma, and in my mind reincarnation and karma don't really mesh with Christianity's depiction of heaven and hell. That's now; however, up until 1986, I fervently believed in heaven and hell. In fact, I was terrified by the thought of hell. One day back in 1982, my very dear friend and then boss, Neil Whitehouse, and I were grabbing some lunch when the subject of my religious beliefs came up. I was very much "born again" at that time of my life.

When I voiced my fear of hell, Neil looked me in the eyes and asked, "Why do you believe in hell?"

He wasn't judging me; he didn't try to change my mind. He simply asked the question, listened to my answer, and said no more.

A few years later, as I began to seriously question whether the Bible was God's word or mankind's effort to control mankind, I often thought back to that moment, and how simplistic and unquestioning my answer was: "Neil! It's in the Bible, so it has to be true!" Does the Bible talk about hell, or is it something that I learned about during church services?

After Gilbert dictated the above material, I decided to do some research into this subject, and I found website after website with many interesting arguments both for and against the existence of hell. I found many sites that indicated that that the word "hell" is not used in approximately two-thirds of the Bible, which, if true, is something I perceive as very telling. I think it all boils down to the accuracy of the translations, and it would be very easy to manipulate a translation to achieve one's personal goals. Unless we read the original text in the original language, how can know for sure what was actually written?

I've often read that during the first Council of Nicaea, which took place in 325 AD, Emperor Constantine and a council of Christian Bishops made decisions regarding what would be included in Christian doctrine (resulting in the first uniform Christian doctrine), which books would become part of the Bible, and the settlement of a debate regarding the divinity of Jesus Christ. I'm just contemplating here, and let's ponder this thought together: IF these are indeed the things that took place at the Council of Nicea, is it such a big stretch to entertain the idea that certain subjects (i.e. reincarnation and karma) could have been left out and the concept of hell added in?

Why would they do such a thing? Because it's hard to control the population if they know they are responsible for their own souls and much easier to control the population if they think they will suffer in fire and brimstone for eternity if they *don't follow the rules* decided on by a council of men?

In an online article called "Honest Questions and Answers About Hell" written by Mercy Aiken and Gary Amirault, they make a compelling argument against the concept of hell, and some of their points definitely made me go "hmmm" when I read them. To start, they wrote that "Two thirds of the Bible (the Old Testament) does not mention hell at all" and that "Sheol," the Old Testament word that is sometimes translated as "hell," actually means "grave" by definition. According to Maiken and Amirault, Sheol was

145

"where everyone in the Old Testament went when they died—good or evil, Jew or Gentile."

I found several other websites that also discuss the correct definition of the word Sheol. In addition, Aiken and Amiralut went on to ask the following questions:

1. Why didn't God mention hell in the beginning of the Bible? God said the penalty for eating of the Tree of Knowledge of Good and Evil was death—not "eternal life" in fire and brimstone;
2. Why wasn't Cain, or Sodom and Gomorrah, or any of those who committed the earliest recorded sins warned about hell?
3. Why didn't Moses include a warning about hell as punishment for breaking the Ten Commandments?

No one wants to read the Word of God more than me—and the concept of hell and why we would be sent there is at the core of my search for the truth. Those of you who read my book *Windows of Opportunity* know that I began asking questions when a pastor told me that my family would be going to hell. Their sin? He said that they practiced idolatry because some of them had statues of the Virgin Mary in their houses and yards and/or wore crosses with Jesus on them. Several of those relatives have passed over to the other side, and I've had contact with them through automatic writing—I know that they did not go to hell.

And now that I've gotten started, someone please write and tell me why, why would God create us only to make us suffer for eternity in fire and brimstone if we commit a *sin*? And to be forgiven for a *sin*, why would we need to go through another human being instead of talking with God directly? As a means of righting wrongs and rewarding good deeds, the law of karma seems more plausible to me and more of what I would expect from a loving Creator/God.

146

SECTION SEVEN:

Raising Our Vibrations

Chapter Twenty-Seven:

We CAN Do It!

Hopefully by the time you are reading this section, you have recognized just how powerful you are and realize that together we have, can, and will continue to have a major impact on raising our planet's vibrational level so we can minimize the overall effects of the Shift. It's in our hands— well, it's actually in our thoughts, words, and deeds. The following message is from Gilbert and the Group:

Sherri, today we will continue our discussion of the 2012 phenomenon. First and foremost, know that there is no exact date or time for the Shift to complete. Some will Shift with the planet and others will not— this is nothing to worry about or be upset about, for all is as it should be. Some will feel badly for those left behind but they are not really being left behind. They are simply on another path at another level of growth and development. The decision to Shift or not Shift has been made already by everyone who is currently incarnated, and it's a decision that has been made by each individual entity. Subconsciously, everyone on this planet knows if they are Shifting or staying. Each individual on this planet is in a position to assist in the Shift to make it easier for all— Starseeds, Lightworkers, those who will transition, and those who will stay—all **can** *and* **will** *make a* *difference.*

Chapter Twenty-Eight:

Six Easy Steps to Generate More Positive Energy

Gilbert and the Group are nothing if not pragmatic, and they've dictated a list of suggestions for us on how we can work on raising our vibrations. As I received these suggestions, I recall thinking, *"Geez, I think we know this stuff already!"* I know that some of this was given to us in *Windows of Opportunity*. I was quickly reminded that it will take a bit of time for some of us to embed these action items into our everyday lives and make them a habit; therefore, they bear repeating. I was also reminded that since *I* have yet to incorporate all of these positive energy items into my daily routine that I should pay great attention to what was being dictated. Answers.com says it takes 30-40 repetitions to make something a habit, so I guess I shouldn't roll my eyes when I'm asked to repeat something.

I do know from experience that the simplest things are often the hardest to put into action, and I am, admittedly, living proof of that. It's work to change old habits and develop new, more positive ones.

The following suggestions from Gilbert and the Group are presented exactly as they came through, but I have put the information into paragraph form and numbered them to make the information easier to read.

1. <u>*Stop judging each other*</u>. *We have talked about this ad infinitum because it is like a power plant exploding negative energy into the atmosphere each and every day. On your side of the veil you do not know the 'whats' and 'whys' of anyone's life plan. Thus, you are in no position to stand in judgment.*

2. <u>*Watch what you think, what you say, and what you do at this very important time*</u>. *The more positive energy that is put out there, the better off <u>all</u> will be. It is very important for all to start to monitor their thoughts because thoughts are extremely powerful. There is nothing that exists that wasn't first a thought and nothing that has happened that wasn't first a thought. Things manifest more slowly on the planet Earth than in other places, but they still manifest. Sherri, you have seen this yourself with things you've wished you had that suddenly appeared. Those were pleasant surprises, my dear, but the reverberation of negative thoughts and vibrations is not so pleasant. As many will see, thoughts are materializing at a much faster rate, and all must watch their thoughts and words—we cannot emphasize this to you enough.*

3. <u>*Be positive in the face of adversity*</u>. *When adverse circumstances present themselves or something occurs that causes grief, examine them for Windows of Opportunity and Relationship Villains. Try to understand that they are part of the overall life plan of many individuals. We need not understand another's life plan or even our own to know that there is something greater than ourselves at work.*

4. <u>*Look for ways to bring more light to the planet*</u>. *This can be done in baby steps with big results.*

    a. *Stop gossiping—it is not good for anyone.*

152

b. *Stop being rude-- it spews negativity into the atmosphere.*

c. *Stop plotting against others—these dramas do no one any good and add to the negativity in the atmosphere.*

d. *Stop looking for underlying insults in what other people say to you and stop insulting other people. All are on their individual path, and you don't know what it is. Just because others may not meet your current standards does not make them wrong.*

5. *Start looking for ways to be nice to people— including but not limited to these actions:*

a. *Greeting people in a friendly way. Saying good morning, good afternoon, and good evening when you see people.*

b. *Smiling at everyone you see—not a crazy person smile, Sherri, as you would say—but a nice smile or even a half smile will help, as long as it is genuine. Smiling perks people up, and both the one who is doing the smiling and the one who is smiled at will feel a boost of positive energy from this simple yet powerful act.*

c. *Say nice things when appropriate. If you can say something nice to someone in a sincere way, then do it. Look for things that you admire about others and give them a compliment. Both the person saying it and the person receiving the kind words will benefit with a burst of positive energy.*

d. *Hold the door open for others when they need it. This is a simple and easy act that*

153

takes no time but carries a positive energy bang.

e. *Give someone else the parking spot when two of you are trying to get it at the same time. It is the little things like this that you can do every day without taking any time that will help you hold the light while you send out positive energy and make room for more light to enter.*

6. *Stop sweating the small stuff. If people cut you off in traffic or beep their horn at you, don't give in to the negativity of the moment. Look at these moments as challenges to hold the light. Stay positive and examine them for Windows of Opportunity. When we return negativity in moments like these, we dim our light. Part of the challenge is to maintain your current level of light while bringing in more light and sharing that light via positive thoughts, words, and actions with those around us.*

Here's a quick note regarding smiling. My friend, Shelly, was at a Farmer's Market in Santa Fe, NM, in June 2010, where she smiled at a vendor. She was surprised when he thanked her for "gifting him with her smile." A smile is a gift! And it's one that costs us nothing, so we can all afford to give them out all day long. Gilbert and the Group completed this list with the following advice:

And here is what will happen when YOU put these things into practice and they become habit. YOU will change. YOU will become a nicer person. YOUR vibrational level will rise. YOU will find more opportunities for growth. People will want to be around YOU more because they will sense the light within YOU. YOU will be helping the planet complete

the Shift in an easier manner, and YOU will be taking steps toward becoming a fifth-dimensional being.

Since receiving this dictation, I have become more aware of opportunities to "be nice" and "turn the other cheek" as they are happening, which *does* make it easier to make a conscious behavioral choice. Awareness is important, but action is key. Let me share with you the plan of action I made for myself after being scolded by Gilbert when I said I already knew all this stuff.

I started with the item that was the easiest for me to incorporate into my daily life and practiced it every day to help turn it into a habit. As I master one item, I'm throwing all of my attention on the next easiest item. Eventually I'll incorporate the ones I find more challenging. Actually, I've found myself chipping away at the challenging ones as I'm working on the changes I thought would be easiest.

Like me, you're probably wondering if such small things truly have an impact—let me share with you what I've accomplished so far.

I started with #5 above—each of those little steps seemed immediately "do-able" to me, and I started by expanding my "smiling skills." I found that it is very easy for me to smile at people and, oh my gosh, wait until you start doing this and see the look on people's faces! They really DO smile back! Sometimes it looks like they don't really want to, and/or they have a look of confusion as they're smiling back—which makes me smile bigger! I've been smiling at people I know and at strangers for a good six months now, and I have yet to smile at someone who didn't return the smile. If you read my book *Windows of Opportunity*, you already know that I started smiling at people in the grocery store, where I was continually bombarded by rude people and experienced a great deal of cart rage before I realized that I was contributing greatly to what was going on at the corner Albertson's. I've now expanded my smiling to include the following: 1) anyone

155

walking past me as I'm walking into a store or a building; 2) everyone in the hallways at work; 3) everyone who walks into my office; 4) anyone who approaches me anywhere; and 5) while talking on the phone. I think it makes my tone of voice sound friendlier! As I walk into rooms and offices, I look around at everyone present, smile, and say hello. And it *is* contagious. People smile back, and I do feel happier as I'm smiling at them.

The parking spot thing was easy for me because I don't care about getting the closest spot. I just want to park and get in and out of the store—I'm always in a hurry! But my friend, Heidi, and my husband, Ted, love to circle the parking lot looking for the closest spot they can find. I've been in cars with them many times as they circled the parking lot five times or more to find the "perfect" spot, pull in, and then want to move the car because they see a car pull out of spot that's closer to the front door. And they do move the car to that closer spot! Believe me when I say that I could be in and out of the store before they settle on the perfect spot to park. I used to make smart-alecky comments to both of them when they did this, but now I just chill and enjoy the ride. When I first tried keeping my mouth shut about their parking habits, I was almost literally biting my lip, but it got easier as time went on. And as I'm typing this, I just realized that for me, this is also a step towards "Watching what you say" in #2 and "Not sweating the small stuff" in #6. It's epiphany time for me right now as I realize how much negative energy I was spewing into the atmosphere with my snarky little parking comments. Now that I've stopped the comments, the next step is to say things like, "Nice parking spot"—but I have to wait until I can mean it when I say it!

For me, "greeting people" happened naturally and coincided with my adventures in smiling! They kind of go hand in hand. Holding the door open for people was also easy for me, and I love, love, love the look on men's faces as they realize a woman is holding the door for them and insisting they go first. At first they don't want to move, and I say, "It's 2011! It's okay!" and then they look at me and smile or laugh! So these little things really do work.

And the part of #5 that I'm most proud of accomplishing is finding something nice to say to people. It has to be genuine, or it's counterproductive to creating positive energy and sharing the light. I've found that it's surprisingly easy to find something nice to say. First of all, unless you are living in or visiting a nudist colony, everyone we see has clothes on, right? That means there are lots of options where we can give a genuine compliment, such as saying, "Nice shirt/slacks/skirt/dress/shoes/socks/necklace/hat/etc. I know this stuff works because shortly after I decided to concentrate on the stuff listed in #5, someone stopped me in the hall at work and told me that my eyes were beautiful—and I was on cloud nine for the rest of the day! I still think my Guide Group staged that for my benefit to prove their point, and their point was well made. I felt great after getting that unsolicited compliment, and I wanted to make other people feel great, too. My friend, Mary, recently e-mailed me about her experiences in this regard.

> *I'm finding myself showing strangers I care more, such as when a cashier at the grocery store is checking groceries out, I ask how his/her day is. Asking about them and how they are personally doing really freaks some of them out, and they respond often in detail. You know they feel uplifted because a stranger asked about them personally.*

It just takes a very little bit of time and effort to make someone's day.

Working on #3, "Be positive in the face of adversity," has not come quite as easily for me. When I took those pay cuts at work, I obsessed over each one of them and to be quite blunt, I ranted and raved and yelled and screamed and complained about those cuts even though deep down I knew that the changes at work would force me to open up to new opportunities. Because of those cuts, I've started successful jewelry and workshop businesses, but when I was initially facing with that adversity, I was not pleasant to be around. Looking back, I know there were better ways to share my feelings with my friends and family. They would have been just as supportive, and I wouldn't have deposited so much negative energy into the atmosphere. I think I missed a Window of Opportunity or two for growth, and hopefully the next time I'm faced with adversity, I will face it in a calmer, more *Lightworker-like* manner.

Chapter Twenty-Nine:

11 Things You Can Do Today to Raise Your Vibrations

Gilbert and the Group have more insights and suggestions for us. Although some of it is slightly repetitive, Gilbert and the Group requested that all of it be included. This information was dictated over a period of several weeks and interspersed with other dictation. I've done my best to take random sentences of dictation and put them in a format that makes sense and will help the Group get their points across. The following words are those of Gilbert and the Group—the order is mine.

There are many things to understand about the Shift. Those who Shift with the planet will have a different type of body than they do now. This is something that will happen automatically and is part of evolution. We spoke of the evolution of the human race with you before [see Windows of Opportunity] and this is part of that evolution. Human beings will continue to evolve further than what will happen during this Shift since it is just one stage of your evolution as a species. Even though the Shift is fraught with hardships, the citizens of the planet Earth can help. We have been over this before and ask again that all thoughts and words be carefully monitored so that less and less negativity is put into the atmosphere. Random acts of kindness are a must, and you will see a change in people as these things are put into practice. Even through the weather disturbances, as religions undergo their changes and Shift to the spiritual, and changes take place in business and banking, you can make a difference by keeping your eyes on the prize. You WILL make a difference by being positive in all you do, especially in the face of the adversity that is here now and is coming.

For those who wish to make a conscious effort to raise their vibrations to attract and spread more light and help increase the positive energy on the planet, there are things that can be done immediately. Over time they will raise your vibrational levels and help the planet make an easier transition. The things to be done are really quite simple, and they all have to do with the output of positive energy.

Let us talk more about raising one's vibrations and the things human beings can do to make the transition easier. There are so many ways that one can go about it, and really, they all revolve around the old adage, "Do unto others as you would have them do unto you." As more beings adopt and practice this philosophy, positive changes will happen for all. What if everyone would take these actions?

✓ *PRACTICE ACTS OF KINDNESS. Doing so will create an immense outpouring of positive energy into the atmosphere. The term 'random acts of kindness' is interesting because it indicates that the kindness bestowed is not pre-meditated or pre-planned—it is entirely spur of the moment, or more importantly, those involved are completely 'in the moment.' During a random act of kindness, no one is thinking about the past or the future, they are having an exchange that is firmly in the present and has their attention focused in the present. That is a great thing because so many have a hard time living in the moment, living in the present. With an act of kindness you are a lighthouse emanating positive energy—you create a positive field around you and the person you are in contact with. This positive energy continues to emanate around you and positively affects others that you come into contact with, creating a domino effect. So random acts of kindness—seeing things that need to be done to help people, to help animals, to help the planet and then acting on what you perceive, well, that's a dynamic way to increase vibrational levels.*

✓ *SMILE! We know that we've talked about this before, but if you think about it, you will realize that the smallest smile yields big results. When you smile at people, they cannot help but smile back; when they do, they release endorphins in their body. They become happier. Even if it's just a little bit, it is enough to decrease negativity within that person and for the planet. Not only are the original smiler and smilee affected, but everyone they come into contact with that day will feel better (smiles are healing) and benefit from their positive vibrations. With no effort, they will share in it, adding their own positive energy to the atmosphere and sharing their smiles with others around them. A smile is a small thing, but it is has a very big charge to it. If everyone would start smiling more, they would help raise their vibrational level while helping others and the planet at the same time.*

✓ *PAY ATTENTION TO YOUR THOUGHTS AND WORDS. Continue to pay great attention to your thoughts and words. They will manifest quickly and can do great damage or great good. It is important again to reiterate that thoughts are things and will come into being much more quickly now and especially after the Shift, which is why only those of the correct vibration and mindset will make the transition. If those who continue to think and talk about violent acts were to make the transition, can you imagine what would go on if their thoughts and words immediately became reality? That cannot and will not be allowed to happen. Getting your thoughts and words under control will help you raise your vibrational level.*

✓ *HOLD A POSITIVE ATTITUDE. Show appreciation for the things you have. Don't moan and groan about things you wish you had. If you want something, put it out to the universe. It will come to you—that is the way of the universe. Begin now to understand that you are powerful, and what you desire is what you will manifest. You have the power to change things. Moaning and groaning are negative. Telling the universe what you desire is positive.*

✓ *TAKE CARE OF MOTHER EARTH. Take care of this planet! Just because a Shift is happening does not mean that Earth is a garbage can! Clean up after yourself and clean up after others if that is what it takes to keep the Earth clean. Littering is not allowed! Dumping toxic waste is not allowed! We also want to address the way people treat the oceans and the beaches—no garbage should be dumped into the ocean. People should pick up their garbage from the beaches. We also want to say that trees should not be eliminated unless absolutely necessary because they are a part of environment. Chopping down trees for no reason is not a positive act.*

✓ *GET INTO THE RECYCLING HABIT. Recycle as much as possible. Try and find different uses for everyday things that would normally be thrown away because even just the act of thinking about this will affect your vibrational frequency in a positive way.*

✓ *TEACH YOUR CHILDREN TO LOVE EARTH. Talk to and teach your children. Children are open to learning new things. They can be taught to think and act in a 'New Age' way that will cause less damage to the planet.*

✓ *HELP THOSE IN NEED. We want to say that if one adopts the practice of helping people they see in distress, like helping someone change a tire, for instance, such acts are lightning rods for bringing in more light and creating positive energy. Another way to draw light is to do positive things such as helping people who are in need. Help charitable causes that you feel a pull toward. That doesn't necessarily mean giving money. Giving your time can make a huge difference.*

✓ *BE KIND TO ANIMALS. We also want to address the fact that being kind to animals of all kinds, not just domesticated animals will also help. Feeding birds and squirrels and other wildlife that have lost their habitat is not a crazy thing to do. In fact, it is a wonderful thing to do, and it will help increase your vibrations and those of the people around you. The animal kingdom has been severely abused. The time is now to be kind to those wild creatures who are around you and give them a helping hand as they are in need of food and water just as human beings are in need of food and water. They are losing their shelters. They will adapt as well as they can, but a helping hand in this way will draw more light to the planet and create positive energy.*

✓ *STAND IN THE LIGHT AND LET NOTHING DETER YOU. Another thing that people can do to increase positive energy and vibrations is to stand up for themselves and make their own choices. Not allowing others to bully them or impede their freewill is a very big step, not only toward working out karma, which may exist from such circumstances but also toward increasing their vibrational level as they stand strong in their power.*

✓ *BE AWARE OF EVERYTHING AND EVERYONE. One of the reasons entities continually reincarnate is to pay karmic debts, and with each debt paid, you begin to vibrate at a higher level. For this reason, looking for life scripts and Windows of Opportunity and taking action in these areas will speed the elevation of your vibrational level.*

It's interesting, isn't it, how basic this information is? It reminds me of the book *All I Really Need to Know I learned in Kindergarten* by Robert Fulghum because there is nothing here that is difficult to do. It's all elementary school stuff.

In the beginning of this chapter and in other places throughout the book, the Guides mention a new *light body* that we will have when we transition. A description of the *light body* is included in Chapter Thirty-Eight.

We've reached the end of the actual list of things to do, but Gilbert and the group have more advice for us:

> *Sherri, as those present on the planet begin to take action to increase their vibrations and attract more light, it will still take courage and determination to make changes in their lives. Taking action is always more difficult than standing still and waiting for things to happen, but to make the Shift easier for all concerned, action must to be taken.*
>
> *A thorough examination of one's habits and ways of acting and reacting will be the first step. After one writes down all of the things they think they should change or know they need to change, the next step is to review that list and choose the easiest one or two things to do first. Doing one thing on the list will propel you to do another and another because making progress will provide the motivation to continue. Soon the easiest ones will be gone from the list, progress will be made, and the bigger challenges on the list can be conquered.*

As you already know, I did make an actual list that included all the items in #5 under the Six Easy Steps part of Chapter Twenty-Eight. I chose those things because they seemed like the easiest ones for me to work on and make progress with quickly. My "day job" includes Sales Training, and as such, I continually encourage sales reps to write down their goals and tape them to their bathroom mirror or some other place where they'll read them every day. Reading and reciting your goals or affirmations aloud when you get up in the morning and when you go to bed at night is a great way to communicate with the Universe. The Universe gives us what we tell it we want. The clearer we can be with our goals and desires and the more we focus on what we want, the quicker we will make them a reality.

Throughout this book, we've talked about how important words and thoughts are, and in Chapter Seven we talked about using our words wisely. This talk about how powerful our words and thoughts are is not something that is just starting to be channeled and talked about now that we are firmly in the midst of the Shift. In the 1920's, a brilliant metaphysician named Florence Scovel Shinn wrote *The Game of Life, Your Word is Your Wand, The Power of the Spoken Word, The Secret Door to Success,* and several other books that are centered around this principle. Her books are still available today, and I highly recommend them because they show us how to think and speak more positively as we communicate our true desires to the Universe. In Shinn's words, "Man has the power to change an unhappy condition by waving over it the wand of his word." She wrote those books **80 years ago**, but the way the Universe works hasn't changed! What happens to us always comes back to what we've planned for ourselves and what we've communicated to the Universe. Each of us is an incredibly powerful being—and with our thoughts, words, and actions, we communicate to the Universe what we want. I am fascinated by the fact that nearly a century ago, Florence Shinn was writing about the same stuff that Gilbert and the Guide Group are dictating to me today. That's how important it is that we understand the power of our thoughts and words. This is something we not only have to get through our heads; it's something we have to take seriously and put into practice.

Setting goals and making a To Do List of what we want to accomplish is an easy way to focus on the things we want to make happen, and it's a great way to start putting more positive energy out into the world. Start by reviewing the suggestions from Gilbert and the Group. Then choose one or two things to work on each month, keeping in mind that each positive change you make, no matter how small, has an impact on your vibrational level. What happened to me will quickly happen to you, too, and you will see how one small change leads to another and another until suddenly you see progress happening in the areas you thought would be the most difficult to tackle.

And remember any change, no matter how small, will send positive energy into the atmosphere, thus affecting the vibrational level in a positive way. There is so much that can be done. We have given simple ways to get started, but there are many more ways still that people can use to increase their personal vibrations. Our list is nothing more than a beginning, and lists are nothing more than lists. It's action that must be taken to move this process along, so it comes down to freewill and personal responsibility— responsibility to oneself as in living up to a contract to attract and hold the light. This is something that a Lightworker contracts to do. Being responsible to help the planet is another thing a Lightworker contracts to do. It is our hope that Lightworkers will be reminded of their mission when they read these words and make a concerted effort to do more to help the planet. It is not only Lightworkers that can help by completing a 'To Do' list. Every person incarnated currently on the planet can make a big difference. The time is now to start making the little changes because as one person starts to do it, so will others follow. They cannot help but be affected as the positive energy increases around them. Do you understand?

All of the dictation I've received from Gilbert and the Group seems to boil down to the same basic advice: (1) do unto others as you would have them do unto you; and (2) it's the little things that are going to help us achieve our goal, which is an easier Shift. It's almost a David and Goliath kind of thing, isn't it? The Shift is Goliath, and together we are David—and like David's stone, our weapons are small but effective. It is ultimately our positive thoughts, words, and deeds that will allow us to complete this Shift with less drama and pain.

Chapter Thirty:

Arcturian Meditation Exercises

Fifth-dimensional Light: Arcturian Energy Visualization

Sherri, this is Akhnanda and the Arcturians. We are here to give you insight into how to utilize the Great Central Sun to increase your vibrations. The purpose of bringing more light to the planet is to increase the energy level and thus the vibrational level so that human beings will transition to the fifth dimension with less stress.

Creating and maintaining a foothold in the fifth dimension is something that human beings can do for themselves immediately, and it will facilitate the culmination of the transition as we near the completion of the Shift.

Meditating and visualizing oneself as a fifth-dimensional being will create a connection or a gateway, so to speak, to the fifth dimension. The blending of the frequencies will serve to allow your bodies to acclimate to the higher energy while increasing your current vibrational level. Here is a meditation that you can try.

- Lie down or sit up straight in a chair, whichever is most comfortable for you.

- Close your eyes and take 3 or 4 deep, cleansing breaths as you visualize a beautiful, shimmering white light entering your body through the crown chakra at the top of your head.

- Infuse your entire body with this magnificent and radiant light and feel it vibrating within you.

- Feel your body become lighter and visualize it starting to shimmer as you accept the higher energy from the light and begin now to vibrate at this higher frequency.

- Now, begin to visualize and feel yourself beginning to transition and become a fifth-dimensional being.

- Fifth-dimensional energy and the light from the Great Central Sun is surrounding you and within you as you feel and visualize yourself transitioning.

- This is not a stretch of the imagination for you. This is a remembering for you.

- Now feel your new light body separate and step away from your physical body. It looks the same and is the same size, but it is lighter and shimmers with a higher vibration.

- Your consciousness is now present on New Earth.

- As you acclimate to the new sensations of having a light body, try to take a few steps.

- When you feel ready, take yourself on a "walkabout" on New Earth.

  o What do you see to your right? What do you see on your left? What's in front of you?

  o What do you hear?

  o What do you smell?

- Experience the light and the warmth of the Great Central Sun as you explore the world around you, noticing the peacefulness that surrounds you as you gaze at the sites of this beautiful new planet Earth.

- Feelings of love and joy permeate your body as you breathe in the clean, fresh air.

- With each breath you take, feel your energy continue to step up as you breathe in and absorb the light of the Great Central Sun.

- Feel and see yourself shimmering and vibrating as you become a multi-dimensional being once again.

- Continue your "walkabout" for a few more minutes as you take in the sights, sounds, and smells of New Earth.

- Now it's time to bring this fifth-dimensional light, the light of the Great Central Sun, back to your third-dimensional body.

- Visualize your *light body* merging with your current body; your light body looks exactly like your third-dimensional body, only glimmering and shimmering with the light of the Central Sun. They come together easily and fit together perfectly.

- As you visualize the merger of your two bodies, ground yourself knowing that you have connected to a higher energy and merged with the fifth-dimensional light of the Great Central Sun. In so doing, you have increased the frequency with which your body vibrates.

- Slowly now, as you further ground this light into your body in this dimension, begin moving your fingers and hands—then your toes and feet. Stretch and move your body in whatever way you choose.

- When you feel ready, open your eyes, knowing that you are a multi-dimensional being.

[Note from Sherri: Picture your *light body* glimmering with light but otherwise looking exactly like your third-dimensional body. It will make it easier to adjust when you bring your lightbody back into your current body.]

Arcturian Energy Meditation

This meditation exercise was dictated in July 2010 by Akhnanda and the Arcturians. The purpose of this exercise is to accelerate spiritual growth and elevate one's personal vibratory level. In the words of Akhnanda, "As one engages in this meditation, he/she will become more awake to his/her surroundings and thus become more proficient at spotting his/her Windows of Opportunity."

- Prepare to begin the meditation by sitting up straight...or lie down, whichever is more comfortable for you.

- Imagine, visualize, or see a clear white light coming down from the cosmos into your crown chakra, which is located at the very top of your head. Know that you are one with this beautiful white light.

- This white light is the light from which we all emanate and originate. Its source is the Great Central Sun, and it is filled with pleasant and wonderful vibrations of love.

- As you bring the light into your crown chakra, you begin to remember who you are. Feelings of wonder and enlightenment pour over you, both inside and outside of your physical body.

- As you watch and feel the light entering your body, you realize and remember who you are and why you are here. You become open to the Windows of Opportunity that you set in motion for yourself in order to accomplish your goals during this incarnation.

- Continue to envision the light flowing down through your crown chakra, which is now spinning in a most wondrous and luminous way.

- Now feel and see this light as it moves further down your body and enters your third eye. Feel the light as it rests at your 6th chakra, invigorating and energizing your third eye, which is located between your eyebrows.

- Now your third eye chakra is spinning in the same wondrous manner as the crown chakra. Both are spinning together in a clockwise motion. Your third eye is opening more and more as the light provides more energy. This added energy will help you open to your mission and help you spot your Windows of Opportunity as they unfold before you.

- Now follow the light as it travels down to your throat chakra, which is located in the center of your throat near the Adam's apple. This chakra now begins to spin as the light and energy fills and invigorates it with the highest vibration possible.

- Your throat chakra begins to spin, and all three chakras are now spinning together in unison. Now feel the vibrational level of your body increase as you begin to resonate at a higher vibration.

- Feel yourself becoming more and more in tune and at one with this light that flows through you, connecting your crown, third eye, and throat chakras.

- As you feel your vibrations accelerating and your connection to the universe expanding, envision this beautiful white light moving downward now into your heart chakra, which is located in the center of your chest.

- Feel and see the white light as it connects your heart chakra to the others, and together all four chakras are now spinning together in a clockwise motion.

- Feel your heart chakra opening as it never has before. It opens now to new and beautiful possibilities as you remember your purpose for being here and your connection to all humankind.

- All are connected and come together here and now on this beautiful planet Earth to help her heal and move into the energy of the fifth-dimension. As our planet transforms, so too does humankind make the transformation, and together all move forward as one.

- Feel and envision all four chakras whirring in a beautiful motion that allows the white light to increase the frequency of your vibrational level.

- Now allow that light to travel further down your physical body as you begin to ground the changes that are taking place into the here and now. Picture the light as it moves down to your solar plexus and connect this chakra to the other four. Your solar plexus is located an inch or so above your navel.

- Feel your energy level continue to increase as the solar plexus chakra begins to whir and spin. Now take a moment to enjoy the amazing sensation of your escalating vibrational level.

- Feel the sensation in your body as you continue to increase your vibration and open yourself up to see all the possibilities before you. Why are you here? Think about it. What are you here to do? Remember it.

- All will come to you as your vibrational level continues to increase and you become one with the white light from the Great Central Sun.

- Now bring the light further down your body to your sacral chakra, which is located in your lower abdomen. Feel and see this chakra begin to spin and whir with the other five chakras, as you further ground your intention to awaken to your purpose and to your mission.

- Sit in stillness now as you allow yourself to remember who you are and why you are here. No pressure, simply be at one with your Higher Self for a few moments as you receive the information that will help you move forward.

- Now, allow the light, the eternal light of the Great Central Sun, to continue downward into your base or root chakra, which is located at the perineum.

- By connecting now to the root chakra, you ground your intentions for spiritual growth and enlightenment fully into the physical body and onto this plane as you quietly remember who you truly are. You are spirit, you are of the light, and you awaken now to your true nature, mission, and calling.

- As the white light continues to permeate your body and you continue to connect your energy centers with this light, feel the energy surge within you as the light moves you forward vibrationally and spiritually. This is the power of the white light, and this is the power of YOU, the entity presently encased within your physical body. This is who you truly are.

- And now that the light is fully encased in your physical body, slowly begin moving your fingers and hands—then your toes and feet. Stretch and move your body in whatever way you choose.

- When you feel ready, open your eyes, knowing that you will see your Windows of Opportunity quickly, accelerate your spiritual growth, and know your mission and purpose for this incarnation.

Note from Sherri:

When my friend and spiritual guinea pig, Heidi Winkler, tried this meditation for the first time, she was lying down and found it difficult to visualize the light coming *down into her crown chakra*. She had a point. If you do this meditation lying down, envision the light coming into your crown chakra on an angle instead of straight down.

Chapter Thirty-One:

Crystal Vibrations

I have always loved crystals. I love to be surrounded by them, I love to hold them during meditation, and I love to wear them. When I was young and had no extra money at all, I remember saving up to buy a piece of raw amethyst from a little shop in Woodstock, NY. It cost all of $5.00, but that was a lot of money for me to spend back in the 70's when I was working full-time and struggling to put myself through college. I still keep that piece of amethyst next to me while I'm writing, along with dozens more. I love the peaceful feeling that comes from being surrounded by amethyst, quartz, and aventurine. I love the vibrational lift I get from flourite and obsidian. Okay, enough already. I think you get it. I love crystals, so I'm sure you can imagine how ecstatic I was when Gilbert and the Group dictated some information about crystals for this book.

I began studying crystals during the 1980's because I wanted to learn how to work with them to enhance meditation, to help me break through and talk with Spirit, and also to use for healing purposes. I attended a lot of workshops and I learned a lot about the properties of different crystals and stones, but I think I learned the most from Katrina Raphaell's trilogy *Crystal Enlightenment, Crystal Healing,* and *The Crystalline Transmission.* If you could see my copies of these books, you would laugh—they are filled with underlines, notes, and are completely dog-eared! They've definitely seen better days, but they are so worn because I refer to them all the time. After I got these three books in 1990 at a New Age Convention in New York City, I starting going to as many crystal and gem shows as I could get to, looking for pieces of each crystal that Katrina wrote about. I wanted to hold them in my hand and get to know their energy and vibrations as I read about them in the books. Back in the early 1990's, I used Katrina's books to create my own crystal study program, but Katrina now has The Crystal Academy in Hawaii and offers classes in California, on Kauai, and through correspondence courses. Attending classes at The Crystal Academy is definitely on my "bucket list"!

Why did Gilbert want to include information about crystals in this book? Because of their vibrations, of course! Working with crystals helps us increase our vibrational levels. In this chapter, I will share some information about a few of my favorite crystals and stones with the hope that you'll try working with them, too, but first, here's a message from Gilbert and the Group about crystals:

> *Crystal healing is something that is used on many different worlds. In fact, crystals are used as communication mediums and also to power various machinery. Crystals are very powerful as they act as batteries in a way and provide much needed energy to accomplish goals without altering the environment, whether that environment is the body of an incarnated soul or the atmosphere of a planet.*
>
> *The clear and pure energy provided by crystals produces the energy necessary to heal the body naturally, to communicate long distances, and to provide an energy source for vehicles. Crystals are energy packs; they are infused with the energy of the Creator, just as we are sparks of the Creator. So, too, are animals and plants sparks of the Creator. Crystals, rocks, and stones are not what they seem; they also vibrate and are very much part of the world.*

Crystals are imbued with much energy. They are able to assist humankind in healing endeavors, and for the purposes of our current discussions, they are able to assist in raising one's vibrational level. As the purpose of this book is to help people raise their vibrations, we are going to extol the virtues of a few of our favorite crystals, and you, Sherri, can add in your favorites as well.

We are primarily interested in talking about clear quartz and amethyst crystals because they are very powerful and hold their energy very well while simultaneously transferring this energy to the person holding or working with the crystal. They are also here in abundance, and no one is charging ridiculous amounts of money for them. There are expensive boutique crystals available that are powerful and are to be respected. This is true, but for the purpose of raising one's personal vibrations, there is nothing that is as available to everyone and nothing that works so well in so many ways as clear quartz and amethyst. So these are the two crystals that we encourage those who wish to increase their vibrations to work with.

Now for those who wish to open themselves further after working with quartz and amethyst, we suggest moldavite, which is more expensive but a small piece is all that is needed and is supercharged with energy. Moldavite packs a charge that will help jolt one into wakefulness, but it shouldn't be used until after one has experienced the energies of the clear quartz and amethyst. Do you understand? It doesn't make sense to go to something of a more concentrated vibration until one has worked with the general vibrations of the quartz and the amethyst.

Sherri, we very much encourage all who read these words to find and establish relationships with quartz and amethyst crystals. Choosing crystals and working with them daily will help them increase their vibrations, fine tune their energy, and help them to be in contact with their guides and higher selves.

The properties of crystals are communicative, not just for telecommunications on that side of the veil but as a way to facilitate communications between you and your guides. We very much want your readers to understand that there is no need to go through a third-party to receive information. One just needs to be open to communication, and crystals will help open them up. Sherri, it is important for everyone to know that there no reason to hold back when it comes to working with crystals. They are of the light and here on Earth to assist humankind in its evolutionary path.

Gilbert says above that working with clear quartz and amethyst will help open one up to communication with one's guides. This was certainly true for me, but crystals are *not* essential or necessary in order to open up to Spirit. Many people contact their guides and angels without ever touching a single crystal, so please don't feel like you must use crystals in order to make contact.

When I first made contact with my guide, Jeremy, back in the 80's, there were three things going on in my life: (1) I was studying different aspects of psychic development, which helped me open to communication; (2) I was taking a class in meditation at Mount St. Mary College and was practicing my meditation at least twice a day while holding quartz and amethyst pieces; and (3) I got my first piece of moldavite. I ordered a raw moldavite pendant that I put on a chain and wore to meditation class the same day that it came in the mail. During that class, I suddenly started to feel quite "woozy" and a little bit "out of body"—not astral traveling or out of body, just a little out of synch with it. To be perfectly honest, I almost felt a bit of a high. It was definitely a "jolt" to use Gilbert's word. It was just a day or two later that I was able to communicate with Jeremy through automatic writing. I absolutely do believe that moldavite piece (which I still have) helped move me along.

What happened, when I first put that moldavite pendant around my neck was that the vibrations of the stone were much higher than my personal vibrational level, which is why I felt out of sync. My body had to adjust to the vibrational frequency of the moldavite, and in doing so, the moldavite helped my body increase its vibrational level. I had to raise myself up to the frequency of the moldavite. It didn't lessen its level to match me. I'm happy to say that I can now wear moldavite and safely operate heavy machinery without drowsiness or incapacitation! In fact, when I was speaking at Ozark Mountain's 2009 Transformation Conference, Heidi and I each bought a moldavite ring, which we wear all the time—even while driving (!); however, if you choose to work with moldavite, do it from the safety of your favorite couch or chair the first few times you use it as you synchronize your vibrations.

For those of you who might be interested in learning more about moldavite, I'll share with you where I purchased my first raw moldavite pendant, and I see that the company now has a website: www.heavenandearthjewelry.com. At Heaven and Earth, you can also find copies of another book that I have tortured over the years from re-reading it so many times: *Moldavite—Starborn Stone of Transformation* by Robert Simmons & Kathy Warner. This book outlines the scientific and spiritual aspects of moldavite and is very easy to read and understand.

Let's talk next about how to add crystals and stones to your meditation practice, including some information on chakras, and then we'll end this chapter with a description of sixteen stones and crystals to help you get started.

Adding Crystals & Stones to Your Meditation Practice

Holding crystals/stones during meditation and wearing crystal/stone jewelry helps us raise our vibrations for the following reasons:

> (1) the energy(ies) of the crystals/stones merge with our electromagnetic field; and
> (2) the color vibrations of the crystals/stones increase the light force and healing energies around the body.

So meditating with and wearing crystal/stone jewelry helps us achieve a better balance of energy within our bodies while at the same time increasing our overall vibrational level. And...we can choose specific stones to work on specific areas of our bodies to achieve specific goals. It's easy to incorporate crystals and stones into our daily meditation practice.

How to Meditate with Crystals & Stones

1. Choose the crystals/stones that you feel drawn or called to work with;
2. Hold the crystals/stones, wear them, or place them around you where you can see them;
3. Meditate as usual (if you're not sure how to meditate, please see Chapter Thirty Nine).

Crystal Meditation Exercise

Here's a crystal meditation to wake up your higher consciousness centers and attain a greater state of awareness. You'll need a clear quartz point, not a round flat stone. I've been doing this mediation for nearly three decades—it's in the

Crystal Enlightenment book by Katrina Raphael, and it's very easy to do.

- Lie face up.

- Place the terminated point of the clear quartz at the top of your head.

- Meditate as usual.

- To help ground this experience and bring it into physical reality, place an amethyst crystal on your brow (6th/Third Eye chakra) and a citrine crystal on your navel (3rd/Solar Plexus chakra). The amethyst and citrine should be light in weight and on the flatter side so they don't distract you or roll off during your meditation.

Chakra 101: Balance Your Chakras for a Vibrational Lift!

Some of the best information I've read about chakras is at www.spiritualnetwork.net/chakra I highly recommend this website if you feel drawn to learn more about the chakra system. The reason we're discussing chakras in this book is because when our chakras are balanced and functioning properly, we will be able to increase the vibrational level of our bodies. We will feel better, too.

Let's start with some basic information about chakras and then move on to some meditation and balancing exercises.

- o Chakra is the Sanskrit word for wheel, and our chakras are spinning vortexes or wheels of energy throughout our bodies, *and* above and below our bodies. There are many, many chakra points, but we're going to concentrate on the seven primary chakras.

o Our seven major chakras are power points that start at the base of our body and go up through our head. They deal with and help regulate our emotions, spirituality, and health.

o Each chakra is attuned to a different frequency of vibration, color, and sound.

o All colors are vibrations, and using the colors of the chakras in chakra meditations and chakra balancing helps us align and balance them.

o The seven major chakras are these:

> o **First/Root Chakra = Red**. The root chakra is about being physically there and feeling at home in situations. If it is open, you feel grounded, stable, and secure. You feel present in the here and now and connected to your physical body. If you tend to be fearful or nervous, your root chakra is probably under-active. If this chakra is over-active, you may be very materialistic, greedy, or obsessed with being secure and resist change.

> o **Second/Sacrum Chakra = Orange.** The Sacral chakra is about feelings and sexuality. When it is open, your feelings flow freely and are expressed without being over-emotional. You are open to intimacy and have no problems dealing with your sexuality. If you tend to be stiff and unemotional or have a "poker face," the

184

sacral chakra is under-active. You're not very open to people. If this chakra is over-active, you tend to be emotional all the time.

o **Third/Solar Plexus/Navel Chakra = Yellow**. The navel chakra is about asserting yourself in a group. When it is open, you feel in control and you have sufficient self-esteem. When the navel chakra is under-active, you tend to be passive and indecisive. If this chakra is over-active, you are domineering and probably even aggressive.

o **Fourth/Heart Chakra = Green or Pink.** The heart chakra is about love, kindness, and affection. When it is open, you are compassionate and friendly, and you work at harmonious relationships. When your heart chakra is under-active, you are cold and distant.

o **Fifth/Throat Chakra = Blue.** The throat chakra is about self-expression and talking. When it is open, you have no problems expressing yourself. When this chakra is under-active, you tend not to speak much, and you probably are introverted and shy. Not speaking the truth may block this chakra.

o **Sixth/Brow or "Third Eye" Chakra = Purple or Indigo**. The third eye chakra is about insight and visualization. When it is open, you have good intuition. If it is under-active, you may have a challenge thinking for yourself, and you may tend to rely on authorities. If this chakra is over-active, you may live in a world of fantasy too much.

- o **Seventh/Crown Chakra = Clear or Violet**. The crown chakra is about wisdom and being one with the world. When this chakra is open, you are unprejudiced and quite aware of the world and yourself. If it is under-active, you're not very aware of spirituality. If this chakra is over-active, you are probably intellectualizing things too much and may be ignoring your body's needs.

- o Each chakra needs to function independently at its proper frequency. **When all of the chakras are vibrating at their correct frequency at the same time, <u>the entire physical vibration of the human body will be increased.</u>**

- o When our chakras are blocked or not functioning properly, we can't move to a higher level and our connection to spirit is blocked. This can make us feel depressed, unhappy, and even angry.

- o When our chakras are open and functioning properly, energy flows through them, and we're in balance. We're ready to connect and communicate with spirit. And we feel very happy!

Chakra Balancing Exercise

Here's the bottom line on chakra balancing. Interaction between the stones and chakras will bring the chakras into a healthy balance/vibration and heal the part of the body that is out of balance. Placing a different stone on each of the seven chakras acts as a general tonic to strengthen and tone your entire system; the colors of the stones give each chakra a vibrational boost. This will bring each chakra and the entire chakra system into harmony.

o Choose stones in the chakra colors (see list below) that you're attracted to, or that call to you. Place one or two of the same color range on each chakra center; i.e., reds on the 1st chakra, oranges on the 2nd chakra, etc. Small tumbled stones work very well and are inexpensive. Hint: flatter stones will stay where you put them, and lighter stones won't start to feel heavy and uncomfortable once you place them on your body.

o Lie on your back and make sure you are comfortable and warm.

o Place the stones on the lowest chakra first and move upwards.

> o **Root Chakra (1st):** Choose a red stone/s and put it/them near the base of the spine or use two red stones of the same type and place one near the top of each leg.
>
> o **Sacrum Chakra (2nd):** Choose an orange stone/s and put it/them on the lower abdomen.
>
> o **Solar plexus/Navel (3rd)** Choose a yellow stone/s and place it/them between the navel and the ribcage.
>
> o **Heart Chakra (4th)** Choose a green or pink stone/s and place it/them on the center of the chest. You can also add a pink stone/s for emotional clearing/healing.

187

- **Throat chakra (5th)** Choose a blue stone/s and place it at the base of the throat at the top of the breastbone.

- **Brow/Third Eye chakra** (6th) Choose a purple or indigo stone and place it on the center of the forehead. You can also use a dark blue stone.

- **Crown chakra** (7th) Use clear quartz or violet stone or crystal on the crown just at the top of the head. If you use **amethyst** for the brow, use a **clear quartz** stone at the crown. If you can use a **dark blue stone** at the brow, use a **violet stone** at the crown. I tend towards amethyst and clear quartz, but this is personal preference.

- Start with the first chakra and visualize it spinning. Feel its energy as it starts to heal your body. Repeat with each individual chakra until you have visualized all seven chakras. Spend at least a minute or two on each chakra.

- This balancing exercise can be done in ten minutes or can last for more than an hour. Trust your instinct and intuition (you know—that little voice we keep talking about!). For the first time, I would plan for at least forty minutes and try to spend five minutes on each chakra.

- How do you know something's happening? Everyone is different, but some of the things you might feel include the stones turning from cold to hot or from hot to cold. You might feel a buzzing or vibration in your body, or you might feel nothing at all. Regardless of what you do or don't feel, the stones are doing their job, and you will feel better and happier when you finish your session.

o When removing the stones, always remove the highest one first, leaving the lowest stone last. (I'm not sure why we do it this way, but this is the way I learned it.)

o Cleanse your stones by holding them under running water for a minute and then place them in the sun to dry. [Note: cleanse your stones after doing this exercise; also cleanse your stones if someone else handles them because they absorb energy from whoever is holding or working with them.]

Chakra Meditation Exercise

o **Assume your meditation posture**, making sure to keep your back straight to ensure energy flow throughout your body.

o **Regulate your breathing[1]**

o **Hold the first chakra (root) meditation stone in your hand.** Imagine its color as clearly as possible and focus on this chakra.

---

[1] "Yoga Breathing" works very well for the chakra meditation. Pretend you're filling up a party balloon on your belly. Inhale by filling the abdomen with air and continue inhaling as you expand and fill the chest. Then exhale first from the chest as it empties and falls and then continue exhaling from the abdomen as it draws inwards completely. This is one round of full yoga breath. Don't force it—your breath should flow fully and naturally.

- o **Visualize the color of the stone entering you through its chakra point** on the body. Then visualize it expanding and permeating your body.

- o **Place the stone on** or touch any part of your body that needs this stone's/crystal's healing energy.

- o **Repeat for each of the 7 major chakras.**

Sixteen Crystals & Stones to Help You Get Started

As you read earlier, I've been instructed by Gilbert to include some information about the properties of clear quartz and amethyst in this chapter. I've also included descriptions of a few other crystals and stones that I personally use to help you get started. There are lots more out there. What follows is a very basic and general overview. There is much, much more to learn and know about each of these powerful crystals and stones if you are so inclined. You can study them in-depth online, and/or you can order my three favorite Katrina Raphaell crystal books through her website.

Many of the crystals and stones below come in different colors, but I've zoned in on one particular color for meditation and chakra-balancing purposes. I've also indicated which chakra center the stones are associated with to make it easier for you to choose which stones you want to work with when you try the exercises outlined above.

- • **Quartz (Clear) [Seventh/Crown Chakra]** Clear quartz radiates the Divine white light and allows the user to work with that light. It's a receiver, amplifier, conductor, and generator of energy. It is used for meditation, transformation, stability, knowledge, protection, healing, and enlightenment. It is an

190

important tool for communication with the spiritual world, and it helps open psychic centers, thus enabling the ability to meditate more deeply. It helps one to release the higher consciousness and is particularly helpful when used during meditation or when working to contact or align with one's Higher Self. This is the first crystal that I ever picked up and held in my hand.

- **Amethyst (Purple) [Seventh/Crown Chakra or Sixth/Third Eye Chakra]** One of the best stones for meditation, amethyst works especially well when placed over the third eye. A meditative and calming stone, it works in the emotional, spiritual, and physical planes to provide calm, balance, patience, and peace. Emotionally, amethyst can help heal personal losses and grief. Amethyst promotes peacefulness, happiness, and contentment. It also brings emotional stability and inner strength. Amethyst has always been my favorite crystal—I love the color and I love the energy.

- **Flourite** [comes in several colors—you can choose a piece that matches the color of the chakra with which you are working. I typically work with purple and green.] Fluorite amplifies, focuses, expands, and creates new pathways for the mind. In chakra healing, it helps recharge all the areas of the body but is primarily associated with the third eye or the brow chakra (purple flourite) where it helps one reach a meditative state and enhances one's ability to see into separate realities.

- **Turquoise (Blue) [Fifth/Throat Chakra]** This is a stone of peace, serenity and tranquility that increases meditation energy, wisdom, balance, honest communication, strength, friendship and love. In healing, this stone connects the spiritual bodies with the other levels: the physical, emotional, and intellectual. My friend, Linda Conklin, loves to wear turquoise jewelry. I wear turquoise when I want to communicate well. Don't laugh, but I nearly always have it on when I do a radio show, lecture, or workshop.

- **Lapis Lazuli (Blue) [Fifth/Throat Chakra]** This stone enhances awareness, insight, and intellect. Lapis strengthens the mind and body and promotes spiritual connection/evolution. Lapis is also used to contact guardian spirits. It's considered to be the stone of truth and friendship. It brings mental clarity and allows us to tap into our inner power.

- **Aventurine (Green) [Fourth/Heart Chakra]** Katrina Raphaell says that this is one of the best stones to use in a crystal healing layout when you want to "soothe a troubled heart, neutralize the emotions, and bring a sense of balance and well-being into the physical body." I frequently use it to balance my heart chakra. Aventurine is an all-purpose healer that is also used to reduce stress and develop confidence.

- **Rose Quartz (Pink) [Fourth/Heart Chakra]** Rose quartz is all about self-fulfillment and inner peace. It's highly recommended for those who are experiencing grief as it helps one express and soothe emotions. Rose quartz opens up the heart to inner peace, self-love, and self-recognition. It is a very healing stone for internal wounds, bitterness, and sorrows. I give rose quartz jewelry to my friends during times of grief, and when my mom passed away, I wore this stone for months to help me work through the grief.

- **Moldavite: (Green) [4ᵗʰ/Heart Chakra]** You already know that I love moldavite. It accelerates spiritual

192

evolution, it's great for chakra activation, and its energy will activate every chakra while clearing blockages. It's wonderful to meditate with and I know from personal experience that it will help you wake up.

- **Yellow Calcite (Yellow) [Third/Solar Plexus Chakra]:** Calcite comes in several colors, and it's a personal favorite of mine. I have a lot of calcite throughout my house. For the third chakra, yellow calcite is the color to use. It stimulates the intellect and is great for an energy boost. It helps you hone your psychic abilities and is great for meditation and channeling.

- **Citrine (Yellow) [Third/Solar Plexus Chakra]:** Citrine is great for dissipating negative energy and can be used to clear negative energies from the body and the environment. It enhances mental clarity, confidence, and willpower while helping to relieve depression, self-doubt, and anger. Citrine is a happy stone and is also thought to promote success, prosperity, and abundance. I love the positive energies of citrine and keep some on my desk at work.

- **Carnelian (Orange) [Second/Sacrum Chakra]:** A great grounding stone that helps with focus and concentration, carnelian helps the mind focus on higher intentions and goals. It enhances analytical abilities and perception. It helps with creativity and inspiration. Oh, and I have to share this with you—it's also said to enhance sexual activity! I use carnelian during focused meditation and chakra balancing.

- **Red/Orange Aventurine (Orange) [Second/Sacrum Chakra]:** All the red aventurine I've purchased is actually a beautiful orange color. Orange/red

193

aventurine stimulates creativity and promotes communication. It's a stone that enhances one's personal power. I find myself wearing a lot of aventurine jewelry, which isn't surprising since most of what I do all day at work is talk to, train, and counsel sales reps.

- **Garnet (Red) [First/Root Chakra]:** According to Katrina Raphaell (and I agree), red garnet "initiates rejuvenation, creativity, regeneration, and blood purification." The red vibration is very powerful and helps when one feels lethargic. It's great for getting your "creative energy" back in line, and oh yes, I can't forget this—it is said to help overcome sexual problems. I keep garnets on my desk when I'm writing—I find garnet to be very energizing.

- **Red Jasper (Red) [First/Root Chakra]** This stone balances the energy and vibrations of the body and eases emotional stress. It's a nurturing stone that provides a source of constant, slow, deliberate energy. It's not the stone to use for a quick energy boost because it works over time. It is very grounding. I use red jasper in my chakra meditations and chakra balancing exercises.

- **Smokey Quartz: [Like Clear Quartz, but with a black or brownish hue] [1st/Root Chakra]** Stimulates and purifies the base chakra and channels/stimulates the energy flow from the crown chakra to the base chakra. Smokey Quartz will gently dissolve and eliminate negative energy and allow positive energies to be re-established. It works to remove blockages, enhance meditation, clarity of thought, and initiate a powerful force-field, which will absorb many forms of negativity, both from within oneself and outer sources. It enables you to follow through with your highest hopes and aspirations and helps you develop increased awareness of psychic dreams and channeling dreams.

- **Black Obsidian: [1st/Root Chakra]** This stone is very powerful and assists those who are searching for the truth. It brings strength and transformation, comfort, truth, and peace. It has the ability to absorb and transform negative energies. It is very grounding. When you first start working with black obsidian, use it in conjunction with clear quartz to help balance its strong energy.

I could take up this entire book writing about different crystals and stones, so let me end this chapter with this advice: don't limit yourself to the crystals and stones mentioned in this section. Go to metaphysical stores and gem shows and see what calls to *you*. One at a time, hold different each crystal in the palm of your hand and close your fist around it. You'll feel the vibrations from the stones you're personally drawn to, and you'll know which ones are meant to go home with you.

Working with crystals and stones is a quick and easy way to raise your vibrations AND there are two side benefits: you'll feel happier and healthier too!

SECTION EIGHT:

What We Eat Matters

Chapter Thirty-Two:

Going "Veggie"

In the chapter about evolution in *Windows of Opportunity*, there is a small section about vegetarianism. In that section, the Guide Group mentions that our evolution as a species includes turning away from killing and eating animals for food, and I talk about how I made the switch to vegetarianism back in the 1980's. Being a vegetarian or vegan has always been an unpopular and difficult lifestyle choice, but there are many signs that the evolution to vegetarianism is in full swing. My sister-in-law, Dawn Burket, of Mishawaka, Indiana, recently went *veggie*, and she shared with me that it's something she's wanted to do since she was a little girl. She told me that she would sit and eat her dinner, getting the meat portion out of the way while trying not to think about where it came from, and then thoroughly enjoying the vegetables on the plate. Dawn, like me, has *gone veggie* because she loves animals and does not want them to be mistreated or slaughtered for her dinner. We just had a conversation recently about the importance of conscious eating, and her statements about the mistreatment of chickens brought tears to my eyes. Dawn was afraid to make the change, just like many of us, but she quickly found that her husband, Doug, and her kids Daniel and Lexi, have been nothing but supportive of her new way of eating. I think that many of us hold back from making the switch to conscious eating because we fear what our friends and family will say and think. I found that after the initial shock, my family and friends came around pretty quickly, and Dawn had immediate acceptance. I believe that Dawn's experience is the new paradigm when it comes to making life changes that also affect our vibrational levels—people are becoming less judgmental and more supportive of a vegetarian lifestyle.

Speaking of conscious eating, I wasn't even familiar with the term until Lightworker Steve Trask, of Atlanta, Georgia, forwarded me a Huffington Post article (www.huffingtonpost.com) titled "Eating Animals: Why Eating Matters," by Kathy Freston. This article was a review of Jonathan Safran Foer's book, *Eating Animals*, and Steve thought I might be interested in taking a look at it—and he was right.

Before reading Foer's book, *Eating Animals*, I first read several more of Kathy Freston's (she is an author, health and wellness expert, and spiritual counselor) Huffington Post articles on eating consciously and eating vegetarian. I was blown away by her honesty and straightforward approach to vegetarian/vegan choices. I was elated to see how she confronted the "you won't get enough protein" myth, and her straightforward, easy to read and understand reporting on how what we eat affects our health and well-being. Ms. Freston clearly and concisely defines *conscious eating* as follows: "Conscious eating means simply this: remaining awake and aware of how food gets to our plate -- and then choosing what we eat according to our values." Conscious eating is all about choosing what we eat, and who among us would knowingly choose cruelty as part of our menu?

There is no doubt in my mind that Kathy Freston is at the forefront of the evolution of humankind and so is Jonathan Safran Foer. *Eating Animals* should be required reading for every single human being on this planet. Mr. Foer has been very clear in various interviews that his book is not a case for vegetarianism—that it is, in fact, a case against factory-farmed meat, and I respect that. Yet as you read his book, you cannot help but question why we continue to mistreat, kill, and eat animals when we now have so many other options available to us. I've repeatedly said that anyone who takes a walk through a slaughterhouse will become a vegetarian, and this book clearly and succinctly conveys the truth about how animals are mistreated before they are cruelly and painfully butchered for our tables. Once we know how animals are treated, we have no choice but to consider the intrinsic moral issues surrounding the killing of animals for food. When you know (and we all KNOW) where meat comes from, how can we continue to eat it once we're aware of the pain and suffering that's part of that hamburger, steak, or chicken dinner? And let's not forget about how that negative energy of pain and suffering is then absorbed into our bodies. I cried my way through this book; I'm crying now as I write this section. I am so grateful and happy that Mr. Foer wrote this book.

In *Windows of Opportunity* I mentioned the old TV show "China Beach" about the Korean War, and how upset I was when I watched an episode where a puppy was butchered for food. Interestingly, Foer addresses the eating of dogs in his book (and pigs, too, who are equally intelligent), and this brings me back to my ongoing question: just who is it that decides it's okay to eat one animal but wrong to eat another? Our eating habits are ingrained in us by our cultures. As human beings evolve, so will our cultures evolve. With this in mind, I'm very happy to share with you an article I recently read in the *Orlando Sentinel* about Korea. Written by John M. Gilonna and Ju-min Park, the headline of the article states **"Koreans Turn from Dog Eating to Owning,"** so you know that got my attention very quickly! According to the article, "Koreans have eaten dogs for centuries, but the habit became more prevalent during the privations that followed the Korean War. It eventually spread from the poor and elderly to be adopted by the more affluent as a niche cuisine." The article went on to say that any protests against eating dogs were dismissed as the unwanted opinions of outsiders, but <u>now</u> South Koreans are taking on a leadership role in promoting animal rights. Lee Won-Bok, who is at the forefront of animal rights movement in Korea, is quoted in the article as saying, "People don't comprehend the suffering these dogs endure...they don't understand what happens to these animals." Won-Bok goes on to say that national laws in Korea prohibit eating dog meat, but the government rarely enforces them, nor does it inspect dog markets for health and sanitary conditions. Won-Bok is also quoted in the article as saying that now *"Koreans are telling Koreans"* to stop the practice of eating dogs—it's not just outsiders sticking their noses into Korean culture anymore.

That sounds like evolution to me; what do you think? It's more than the evolution of individuals. This article is talking about the evolution of an entire culture. This is such a wonderful example of the power we all have to effect change! You place the Lightworkers where they are needed, and they get to work from within—Lightworkers are very much *undercover* and what's happening in Korea is a perfect example of how great change can happen once the light is switched on within a country, culture, or group.

Here is a peak into our post-Shift eating habits and *going veggie* from Gilbert and the Group:

> **There will be new and different types of vegetation and fruits and vegetables, and no one will miss eating animals because those that transition will have moved beyond the need for such things. Their vibrational levels will have moved them beyond such needs, and their bodies will not tolerate it. And those who will apport in the future will certainly be beyond such needs. Those who transition will wonder why they ever ate animals to begin with.**
>
> **A short history lesson is in order here. Human beings were never meant to eat animals. It was an aberration of evolution that the human race started to eat meat**

202

and once they did, they did not turn back. Animals were here first. Human beings are souls encased in a body that evolved from indigenous species and was fine-tuned over time to house incarnating entities. Human beings were meant to SHARE the planet, not brutally use animals for labor and especially not to kill them for food. But as time passed, this aberration in evolution continued, and the soul groups that entered as animals agreed to play the role of a workforce and part of the food chain. All hoped that humankind would see that this was wrong and put themselves back on the original path.

What seems like eons of time on the other side is but decades on this side of the veil, and many are now moving towards the appropriate path when it comes to other life forms on the planet. Those who are vegetarian are brave souls, especially those who led the way. It is not easy to be 'different' on Earth, and many put themselves out there to effect this change and by doing so, brought and continue to bring light to the planet.

Eating vegetarian, or better yet, eating vegan, is something that we can all do right now that will help us raise our own vibrations and raise the frequency of our planet. I'm currently making the progression from vegetarian to vegan. I didn't really plan it; it just seems to be something that is happening as my body is starting to reject certain foods. Suddenly I find that I'm lactose intolerant, so I had to say bye-bye to milk and ice cream (and I loved my ice cream!). At this moment, I'm still eating eggs, and a few years ago I started reading the egg carton labels and will allow only cage free, vegetarian fed, organic eggs into my kitchen.

After reading *Eating Animals* and realizing that even vegetarians need to be more consciously aware of what we eat, I was compelled to do some research into my egg consumption. According to my egg company's website, the hens are "not kept in cages, are free to roam, and are provided with sunlight, shade, shelter, an exercise area, fresh air, and are protected by predators." Sounds great, right? Well, upon further investigation online, I learned that "cage-free" doesn't mean the same thing as "free range" and "free range" doesn't necessarily mean the hens are running around in a beautiful pasture. Are you ready for this? "Cage free" means the hens are walking around in a large building! NOT what I pictured when I read the label on the egg carton.

The company whose eggs I eat note that their egg producers are monitored by the United Egg Producers (UEP) Animal Welfare Program, so I downloaded the *United Egg Producers Animal Husbandry Guidelines for U.S. Egg Laying Flocks, 2010 Edition.* I learned that the UEP is all about the amount of space hens have and the treatment of hens, and I like the fact that someone is watching over the egg producers' shoulders. So far so good, I thought, as I was working my way through the website. I learned that the UEP Guidelines indicate that certified egg producers must score 170 out of 200 points to continue to have certified status, but failure to meet the UEP's guidelines, evidence of backfilling cages, and co-mingling certified and non-certified eggs are cause for failure, regardless of the number of points achieved in the audit. Again, so far so good, and then I read something that made no sense to me at all: **The UEP provides egg companies with seven days' notice before they show up for an audit!** Excuse me???

Once upon a time I was in charge of Mystery Shopping at my company, and believe me, we did not give any notice to the departments we were "shopping." How can you know what's really going on if you give advance notice of a "shop" or 7-day's notice before an audit? This disappoints me and has spurred me forward to find a source of true free-range eggs, or I will give them up completely—what else can I do now that I understand the concept of *Conscious eating* and know that the hens who lay my eggs aren't frolicking around in a sunny meadow?

Since my first book came out, I've had lots of e-mails from readers saying that it's "hard" to be vegetarian, and how do they get protein other than eating peanut butter and rice and beans? There are so many great products on the market now, and they make it very easy to ease meat out of your diet. I am a "lazy vegetarian" and when I get home from work, whatever I make for dinner has to be quick, easy, and convenient. Here are the brand names and websites of some of the products I eat to help you get started. The websites all have tons of recipes for their products and store locators to help you find them.

- Boca Burger (www.bocaburger.com) has so many great products—my niece, Lauren Ihburg, especially loves their Savory Mushroom Mozzarella Veggie Burger.

- Morningstar Farms (www.morningstarfarms.com. My personal favorite is Morningstar's Grillers Prime (the first time I ever ate a Griller, I went back to the freezer to check the box—I thought I misread the label and it was really meat!); I use their Griller Crumbles to make meatloaf and Hamburger Helper; and I use the Chik'n Strips in stir fry. My husband, Ted, who is NOT a vegetarian, actually ASKS me to make the Riblets—he likes them with mashed potatoes and corn on the side! I also like their bacon strips for breakfast and to make BLT's, and my niece, Samantha Seeley (also not a vegetarian, although I have high hopes for the future!) loves their chicken patties.

- Quorn (www.quorn.com). I use their Chik'n Cutlet to make a lot of different dishes that I serve to everyone in my family. I used them to make vegetarian chicken parmesan for Christmas last year and my Aunt Sandra (another non-vegetarian) asked for the recipe and then served it to her non-veggie friends, who didn't know the difference! They also have a turkey roast that is delicious, and I use the leftovers from that roast to make turkey salad for sandwiches.

- Amy's (www.Amyskitchen.com) makes a great line of entrees; their veggie pot pie is one of my favorites, along with their black bean enchilada!

So you see, there are lots and lots of choices, and new and better stuff is coming out all the time. Once you start looking, you'll be surprised at how many great-tasting options there are out there. I've only mentioned a few that I use all the time—the way to find out what you'll like best is by trying different things. And watch for deals! Morningstar Farms has a newsletter you can sign up for that includes coupons, you can do searches online for coupons. Just last week my grocery store had a sale on four different Morningstar Farms products—they were 3 for $10, so I stocked up and saved more than $1 per package. Even vegetarians love a good deal!

Eating "veggie" is much easier now than ever, and I've added a section on my website called The Lazy Vegetarian (That's *me*; I'm the lazy one, not you!), where I post some of my favorite recipes to help you get started. I would love to include some of yours there, too—just e-mail them to me at www.sherricortland.com, and let me know if it's okay to credit you by name with the recipe. I also discovered an excellent cookbook called *Conscious Eating* by Dr. Gabriel Cousens that includes vegetarian recipes and nutritional information. My laziness aside, ideally we want to eat more raw, whole foods, and as little processed food as possible. That's something I'll be working on diligently as I continue down the path *conscious eating*.

Putting aside the concerns about cruelty to animals and the ingestion of fear into our bodies, the point of making changes to our diet is to help raise our vibrational level. We <u>can</u> raise our vibrational level by understanding what we are putting into our bodies and making changes based on that knowledge. How? All food contains energy which vibrates at a certain level, and those energy vibrations from our food are absorbed into our bodies when we eat it. The higher the vibration of the energy in the food we consume, the better we will feel. Our personal vibrational level will rise as we stop consuming food that is latent with fear, chemicals, and possibly disease and start eating more foods that are of a higher vibration to begin with, like fruits and vegetables.

Some folks reading this will no doubt point out the terrible spinach e coli bacteria outbreak during the fall of 2006 as an example of how eating low on the food chain doesn't exempt us from chemicals or disease. I'm right there with you, and, in fact, that was one of the first things that popped into my mind, too, when I started writing this chapter. I checked it out and found that at least 200 people in twenty-six states were affected by that outbreak, and there were three reported deaths. While the exact source of the bacteria was never pinpointed, according to Wikipedia,

> *The California Department of Health Services (CDHS) and U.S. FDA concluded that the probable source of the outbreak was. . . an Angus cattle ranch that had leased land to [the] spinach grower. . . The report found twenty-six samples of E. coli (indistinguishable from the outbreak strain) in water and cattle manure on the. . . ranch, some within a mile from the tainted spinach fields. Although officials could not definitively say how the spinach became contaminated, both*

reports named the presence of wild pigs on the ranch and the proximity of surface waterways to irrigation wells as "potential environmental risk factors." The reports also noted that flaws in the spinach producer's transportation and processing systems could have further spread contamination.

The bottom line on the spinach is that human error caused that outbreak. That occurrence serves as a big wake up call for all of us—if we contaminate our water supply, we will also contaminate our food supply. From what I've read on the subject, many measures have since been taken to improve food safety so this kind of thing doesn't happen again. This is a good reminder that all of us should be aware of where and how our food is grown; that's part of eating consciously. Gilbert and the Group ended their discussion of this subject with the following dictation, which is like music to my vegetarian ears:

There will only be vegetarian animals on the New Earth, you will not find carnivores as that would interfere with the peaceful intentions of New Earth.

Chapter Thirty-Three:

Organic Food

The word *organic* makes anything sound like it's better for you, doesn't it? But just what exactly does *organic* mean? According to the website "Organic Food for Everyone" (www.organic-food-for-everyone.com), organic food is food that has the following characteristics:

- It is produced (grown, stored, processed, packaged, and shipped) with the avoidance of synthetic chemicals, such as a pesticides, antibiotics, fertilizers, and food additives;

- It has no genetically modified food organisms, no irradiation, and no use of sewage, rejected food, or other unpalatable products not fit for consumption;

- Uses farm land that has been free from chemicals for a number of years (usually three or more) and has been tested to prove to be "clean" soil.

According to the website, organic certification procedures require that the food producer and/or distributor keep detailed records and keep the organic food separate from non-organic foods.

Going with that definition, I definitely want more organic food in my diet and I agree with the section on the website that says, "What's healthier for the environment is also healthier for humans, animals, vegetation, and the planet." I wholeheartedly believe organic food is better for us, and I've scrubbed enough wax from grocery-store apples to know that I would buy organic all the time if it were more affordable. It's the cost of organic food that's prohibitive for me and for most of the people I've talked to about this subject.

So, if we're going to spend extra money to eat organic food, how can we be sure the food we're eating is truly organic? I typed "How can you tell if the food you eat is really organic" into my search engine and 28,900,000 websites popped up!

I read a lot of information, none of which gave me a simple answer to my question, but I did find this information: To assure quality and prevent fraud when it comes to organic food, the United States Department of Agriculture has The National Organic Program (NOP) which, according to its website, "Develops, implements, and administers national production, handling, and labeling standards for organic agricultural products."

The NOP also accredits the certifying agents (foreign and domestic) who inspect organic production and handling operations to certify that they meet USDA standards. This sounds great, but thinking back to my egg dilemma, I wanted to know how often the inspections are made and how much advance notice is given for the inspections. I spent a couple of hours going through the NOP website reading about certification, etc., but I couldn't find the frequency of audits. Here's what the Guide Group has to say about organic food:

> *Now Sherri, with regard to organic foods, we are all for them because they provide you with a food source that is not contaminated with pesticides and chemicals. These things have an adverse affect on the body, and this is certainly not news to any living soul on the planet. We mention organic food because if people will eat more organic food, they will allow their bodies to work less hard trying to rid itself of*

chemicals, which leaves the body better able to absorb the light. The planet's vibration level has, is, and will continue to increase as more and more people consciously and unconsciously raise their personal vibrational levels.

As this happens, all who are incarnated on the planet must make adjustments so they can be in harmony with the planet. The less poison ingested by the body, the easier it is for the body to acclimate to higher levels of energy surrounding it—simple yes?

But the expense of organic food is great, and these are difficult economic times for so many. We say this to you: if one can afford it, one should buy it because it is better for the body. That said, if one cannot afford it, then make sure you thoroughly wash your produce because to ingest the chemicals on fruit and vegetables is to cause unnecessary stress to the body as the body seeks to cleanse itself of these chemicals.

Now some can start a little garden either inside their home or outside their home. It may not be a Farmer's Market or cornucopia of organic produce, but any such gardening efforts will go a long way in helping the body to assimilate faster to the increasing energy levels surrounding it.

Apparently, one doesn't have to be incarnated to know that the cost of organic food is a budget-breaker for most of us. Fortunately, Gilbert and the Group are practical and have given us some sound parental advice—wash your food before you eat it!

SECTION NINE:

Alternative Medicine

Chapter Thirty-Four:

Natural Medicine

My interest in natural medicine started when I was still in my 20's. I suffered every month from an extremely painful and debilitating monthly cycle—and the PMS I experienced also led to agony and torture for anyone with the unfortunate luck to be around me at the time. Back then, I was the VP of a small insurance agency in Middletown, NY, and we didn't have a large staff—being late to work or out sick was not an option, and so I sought help from my gynecologist. He prescribed four medications for me to take: one was a painkiller, one was a tranquilizer, another was an antibiotic, and I can't remember what the fourth one was. My gynecologist didn't attempt to help me figure out what was causing my dis-ease. He just wanted to help me mask the symptoms. I definitely wanted the pain to go away, but I certainly was not about to take four medications at the same time. I gave the painkiller a try and quickly learned that if my stomach wasn't full when I took that pill, I became nauseous and endured pain that was worse than the pain I was trying stop. Experiences like that one are what initially led me to look beyond the allopathic medicine that is practiced in the West and look for something more compatible with the human body. Despite what many people think, natural healing methods like herbalism, naturopathy, homeopathy and Ayurveda are compatible with Western medicine; we don't have to choose one over the other.

But I've digressed from suffering—let's get back to my suffering! I went on suffering, and not in silence, until I discovered Edgar Cayce's Association for Research and

Enlightenment (A.R.E). When I joined the A.R.E, I received a free book called the *Individual Reference File*, which is basically excerpts from some of Mr. Cayce's readings. As I was thumbing through the book, I noticed a section about food combinations. The question "What foods should I avoid?" happened to catch my eye (synchronicity). Cayce's answer to this question was: "Rather it is the combination of foods that makes for the disturbance with most physical bodies..." That **really** got my attention, and I kept reading as Cayce talked about the effects of combining alkaline reacting acid fruits with starches (other than whole wheat bread). In several sections of the book, he emphatically repeated the words "And do not have cereals at the same meal with the citrus fruits." That stopped me in my tracks. For at least ten years, I had been eating oatmeal and orange juice for breakfast every single day! After reading Cayce's words, I figured "What the heck," and I switched to grape juice (I couldn't give up the oatmeal!). Very quickly, and I do mean quickly, I started to feel better. I still had PMS, but it wasn't as bad, and I noticed that I wasn't catching cold as often as I had been either.

So for me that one tiny dietary change made a big difference in my overall health and well-being. Because of that experience, I began to study natural medicine and came to understand that pain and discomfort are symptoms of dis-ease—not the dis-ease itself. After that realization, it didn't take long to figure out that the way to save myself from other chronic complaints in my life, like cystitis, would be to find the underlying *cause* of the symptoms I had been putting up with for years.

I went on to read the book *Edgar Cayce on Healing* and discovered the concept of homeostasis, the definition of which is "any self-regulating process by which a biological or mechanical system maintains stability while adjusting to changing conditions." The following is an excerpt from this book, which was written by Mary Ellen Carter and William A. McGarey, and edited by Edgar's son Hugh:

> *Homeostasis in the human body is that balance of energies, functions, and structures that allows the continuity of the life process. It fits into the Cayce concept of things in that homeostasis is the balance that the life force within the body creates so that the spiritual being that we call man might live in this three-dimensional sphere and fulfill the purpose for which he came into being.*

This made an immense amount of sense to me and so began my "formal" studies of herbology, naturopathy, and Ayurvedic medicine. I began studying these forms of natural medicine for two reasons: (1) I wanted to stop being in pain; and (2) I wanted to find the underlying causes of my health problems so I could fix whatever was wrong and stop the recurrence of the symptoms. So what does this have to do with raising one's vibrations, and why am I including this chapter in this book? The reason can be found in the above quote—If our body is out of balance, so is our Spirit, and if that happens, we can't make the progress we came here to make.

In *Windows of Opportunity*, the GG said that we should not drug our children—they were referring to Indigo and Crystal children who are often misdiagnosed with ADD. Gilbert and the Group have more to add to this subject:

> *Sherri, it is important for all to know the underlying cause of symptoms is always an imbalance within the body—there is something causing the body to be off balance. When that balance is restored, so too will health be restored.*
>
> *It does not serve a higher purpose for the body to be continually on drugs. There are times, of course, when it necessary and makes sense to ease one's pain*

and suffering, but it does not make sense to continue to drug oneself instead of trying to find out the core cause of particular symptoms. There is always an underlying cause to a symptom, whether it be headaches or backaches or foot aches. If, like you, one continues to catch colds or develop bladder infections--something is wrong. Something is causing those symptoms, and you are well advised to find the underlying cause rather than settle for constant medication.

Sherri, there are ways to give the body a tune-up so that it does not get out of whack and out of balance. Disease is caused by the body being out of balance. Taking care to keep the body in balance will preempt disease. Once disease has started, it is possible to re-balance the body, and both the symptoms and cause of the disease will depart. There are natural ways to do this rebalancing, and we suggest that you start with those treatments before undertaking massive doses of narcotics and medicines which cause side effects that may be worse than the symptoms originally being treated. We suggest that you consider herbs and natural remedies, massage, acupuncture, and acupressure. We also suggest that you watch your diets because the chemicals in many foods and drinks adversely affect the natural ability of the body to heal itself.

Many medicines cause the mind to cloud and keep the body and mind from being in sync with one another. When this happens, it becomes difficult to hear and listen to that small voice within, which, as you know, is the voice of your Higher Self. Everyone is a channel. You are channels for your Higher Self, which is that part of you not incarnated, the part of your whole that understands the purpose of this incarnation, and the part of you that is trying to be heard in order to help you spot your Windows of Opportunity. You cannot clearly hear the voice within if you are clouded by medicines. Whenever possible, it is better to treat yourself with natural remedies so that they can work **with** *the body, instead of against the body, to cure the underlying cause of your disease and, therefore, alleviate the symptoms.*

I would *never* advise people to stop going to their doctors or stop listening to their doctors' advice. And if you decide to try herbal remedies, you need to make sure that what you're using isn't contraindicated (inadvisable while taking a particular medication because of the possibility of an adverse reaction). Speaking for myself, I will first try natural methods that (1) don't have lots of side effects and (2) won't potentially impair my ability to receive direction from my Higher Self. If I can't get relief (which doesn't happen often), then I'll call my doctor and head over to see her; and I always tell her what I've already tried or happen to be using at that moment so that we can work together to end the dis-ease.

I continue to try natural methods first because I want to do everything possible to expedite my spiritual growth, not impede it. And so in the next two chapters, I will share with you some of my personal experiences with natural healing in the hope that it will inspire you to take a more detailed and closer look at some of the options that are available to us.

Chapter Thirty-Five:

Herbalism

Everything we put into our bodies has a vibrational level, even our medicines, and for that reason, I'd like to talk about herbalism or herbology, which is a traditional form of medicine. Herbalism incorporates the use of plants and plant extracts and is both an art and a science. Herbalism is hardly a New Age medicinal system—in fact, you can find references to the use of medicinal plants in the Bible. Herbalism is, and has been, practiced by many civilizations throughout the ages, including the Western, European, Native American, Chinese, and Indian (Ayurvedic) cultures.

The point of herbalism is to treat the body as a "whole"—to bring the body back into balance, thus eliminating the underlying cause of dis-ease. This is accomplished by combining specific plants and plant extracts to work with the natural energy of our bodies. Different plants have their own individual energy signatures and vibrational levels. By combining different plants and/or their extracts, herbalism seeks to combine the energies of the plants with the energies of the body—to work with, not against, the body as the body works to free itself from dis-ease. Three reasons initially guided me to the study of herbology:

- First, I wanted to be in control of my own healthcare. I was tired of relying on the advice of someone who kept me waiting for two or more hours and then spent all of five minutes with me before prescribing drugs as treatment. Based on what I learned about food combinations from the writings of Edgar Cayce, using medicinal plants to

221

help the body heal itself was a natural next step in taking a management role in my own healthcare.

- Second, I was spending a ton of money on doctor's visits. I wanted to save money.

- Third, I was tired of side effects from over-the-counter and prescription medicines. Most of the time the side effects from the medicines prescribed for me were actually worse than the original symptoms.

I understand that not everyone is as sensitive to medications as I am and may not suffer from side effects at all, but geez, when you listen to those drug commercials on TV where they list all the potential side effects—it's scary. I went online to www.Drugs.com to look up the side effects of some of the medications I've seen advertised on TV lately. Just as a quick example, here are the side effects for a popular allergy medicine I saw a commercial for the other day:

Common side effects might include drowsiness, dry mouth, stomach pain (in children), tiredness, trouble sleeping (in children). Seek medical attention right away if any of these SEVERE side effects occur...severe allergic reactions (rash; hives; itching; difficulty breathing; tightness in the chest; swelling of the mouth, face, lips, or tongue; unusual hoarseness); dark urine; fainting; fast or irregular heartbeat; mental or mood changes; persistent fatigue; seizures; severe dizziness; unusual bruising or bleeding; yellowing of eyes or skin.

Call me crazy, but I think I'd rather have the stuffy nose. Drugs contain herbs and medicinal plants, so why so many side effects from over the counter and prescription medicines? This happens because when drug companies are creating a medicine, they use bits and pieces of a particular plant, not the entire plant. Treating and balancing the whole body requires treatment with whole medicines. When you start messing around with the energy of a medicinal plant, you're playing around with its vibrational level, too, so while you may create something that takes care of masking specific symptoms, the relief from those symptoms may carry a heavy price tag in the form of some ugly side effects. Plus nothing is being done to correct the origin of the problem! So, unless I have no other option, I prefer to ingest the energy and vibrations of the whole plant so that those plant energies can combine with my own energy and help my body balance itself. Everyone knows that whole foods are better for you than processed foods—it's the same principle with medicinal herbs.

When I made the decision to study herbalism, I didn't want a book of recipes. I wanted to understand the properties of different herbs, how and why they worked to balance the body, and how to combine them myself. That's why I chose to study under the guidance of Rosemary Gladstar, who has been a leading herbalist since 1968. Rosemary is the author of several very important books about herbology including, "Herbal Healing for Women" and the "Gladstar Family Herbal." When I discovered that she offered a course called "The Science and Art of Herbology," I knew I had to take it. I think I paid something like $375 for the class materials, and it was the best $375 I've ever spent. It's a home study course. Much to my surprise and delight, Rosemary herself personally graded my homework and projects while also providing feedback and advice. I took Rosemary's course in the early 1990's, and I still refer to the course materials today for information about specific herbs and formulas (You can visit www.SageMountain.com for more information about this great course).

Rosemary has generously granted me permission to share with you some of her teas and remedies that quickly became my personal favorites, and have saved me from a lot of discomfort and wasted money over the years. The formulas included at the end of this chapter are natural remedies that I've used for nearly two decades and I swear by them. As you review the formulas, please keep in mind that an herbal formula isn't something that's just thrown together. The herbs that are utilized are chosen specifically to work together while supporting the body, and as Rosemary teaches her students, "When creating a medicinal herbal formula, there are three cornerstones to every formula." A beginning herbalist needs to understand the basics of creating a formula, and here is a description of the three cornerstones taken directly from Lesson Seven of Rosemary's "The Science and Art of Herbology" course.

- First cornerstone: The primary herb or herbs work directly on the problem and comprise most of the formula. They are the major action herbs in the formula—up to 70% of the herbs used in a formula.

- Second cornerstone: The herb or herbs that support the primary herb/s. They are supportive and nourishing herbs that build, tone, and fortify the body system being worked on with the formula. These herbs have a buffering action in the formula and serve to smooth the sometimes rough or abrasive nature of the primary herb/s— approximately 15-20% of the herbs in a formula.

- Third cornerstone: The catalyst herbs. They activate the body systems being worked on as well as the other herbs in the formula. They serve to activate, stimulate or eliminate—they get things moving—approximately 10-15% of the formula.

Again, the three cornerstone formula makes sense because all the herbs in the formula work together in harmony to support the body. But how do you know which herbs to use for what purpose? Different plants have different energies and uses just like different vitamins and minerals are used to strengthen our bones, help us get over a cold, etc. It just takes time to study and learn what plants work best for which illness. I created a card file to help me keep track of my formulas and to help me find them quickly when I need them fast. Next are the formulas from Rosemary that I promised you, along with some other natural remedies that have worked well for me over the years. [Note: Before trying a formula, check with your doctor and research the herbs for contraindications, particularly if you are not yet an adult, are pregnant or have allergies.]

Burn Salve (Rosemary's Formula)

Rosemary Gladstar discovered the recipe for this salve in a 16th century herbal and modified it to the recipe below. I made my first batch of burn salve in 1993. I made enough to fill two large pickle jars, and over the years, I've given chunks of it to friends who burned themselves taking dinner out of the oven or stayed out in the sun too long. It's great for all first and second-degree burns, sunburns, diaper rash, and cuts and wounds. I have found it to be quite effective when I burn myself with the curling iron! It's February 2010 as I'm writing this section, so the little bit of salve I have left is 17 years old and still works like I just made it. I'm about to make a fresh batch, and when I do, I'll make some extra jars for my friends and family, too. Here's the formula.

- 3 ozs. dried St. John's Wort
- 3 ozs. dried Calendula Flower (Marigold)
- 3 ozs. dried Comfrey
- Olive Oil
- Beeswax (use pure, untreated beeswax that has a golden to golden green color and smells like sweet honey)

Put the herbs into a quart jar glass container and then cover with olive oil so that the olive oil is 2-3 inches over the top of the herbs. Cover the jar tightly and place it in a warm, sunny spot for at least two weeks. Shake the jar daily.

After two weeks, strain the herbs from the oil. For each cup of oil, add ¼ cup of beeswax to thicken the salve. To test the consistency of the salve, put a tablespoon of it in the refrigerator; if it's not thick enough, add more beeswax until you get the desired consistency. Pour the salve into containers with tight-fitting lids and store it in a cool, shaded area.

Bladder Infection/Cystitis (My formula based on Rosemary's teaching)

This tea is a combination of two formulas in Lesson Four of Rosemary's class materials. I did a little experimenting on my own, and once I started making this tea, I never had to pay for medication for this ailment again. By the time I finish the first ¼ cup, I'm starting to feel better. By the third ¼ cup, I forget why I'm drinking it. Oh, I should warn you that it tastes absolutely awful—drinking anything with goldenseal in it is like drinking liquid dirt, but oh so worth it! Here's the recipe.

- 2 parts goldenseal
- 2 parts uva ursi
- 1 part marshmallow
- 1 part pipsissewa
- 4 parts unsweetened cranberry juice
- Make an infusion* with the herbs. Strain and mix tea with cranberry juice. Keep refrigerated. Drink cold or heat it up.

* To make an infusion, pour boiling water over the herbs and let them sit for 20 minutes.

PMS (Rosemary's Teachings and Formula)

Oh, how I suffered with PMS. And so did everyone around me! I learned from the writings of Edgar Cayce about food combinations, and I learned from Rosemary's classes that certain foods contribute to PMS. Changing my diet gave me a lot of relief from the symptoms—I wasn't all sweetness and light, but I wasn't screaming at people anymore. My body was out of balance; here's what I did to help correct it:

- Ate less sugar and white flour;
- Cut out caffeine;
- Cut back on dairy, except yogurt;
- Increased calcium intake with spinach;
- Ate more vegetables;
- And ate more foods that were high in antioxidants and foods high in Vitamins C & E.

In addition, for about six months, I drank the following "tonic tea" every day to nourish the reproductive system. I made it in large batches in a pitcher and drank a cup a day. Make an infusion by pouring boiling water over the herbs, let sit for 20 minutes, then strain and drink. Keep refrigerated until ready to heat it up to drink.

- 2 parts raspberry leaf
- 2 parts strawberry leaf
- 1 part comfrey leaf
- 2 parts nettle
- 2 parts peppermint
- 2 parts lemon grass
- ½ part squaw vine

I also used Bach Rescue Remedy as needed (see the "Stress" section for more about Rescue Remedy).

Cold/Immune System (Rosemary's Teachings/my Formula)

Whenever I start to feel under the weather, I immediately make myself a tea made with 1 part Echinacea (great for the immune system), 1 part goldenseal (nature's antibiotic), and 1 part comfrey (a soothing herb that enhances other herbs). Use one teaspoon of the herb formula per cup of tea, and drink 2-3 cups per day. This tea tastes like dirt, but it is well worth the faces you will make as you take your first sip.

If you can't find the dried herbs to make the tea, you can purchase ready-made Echinacea/goldenseal teabags in health food and grocery stores and you can get them in pill form too, but whenever possible, I prefer to make the tea from scratch. I know there are naysayers who declare that these herbs don't work, but I've found that if I start drinking the tea when cold symptoms first appear and rest for a day, the duration of the illness is very short.

If I don't have any tea on hand, I'll take some zinc tablets, which I've also found work well if I take them at the very beginning of the illness when symptoms first start to appear.

Insomnia (Rosemary's Teachings/My Formula)

I learned about skullcap and valerian in Rosemary's course. A nice cup of skullcap and valerian tea always helps me get a good night's sleep. What I like about skullcap and valerian is that I can get up the next morning and not feel all "fuzzy." You can find skullcap and valerian sleep aides in your local health food store or try my formula: infuse 1 part each skullcap, valerian, chamomile, and lemon balm. I make up a batch as needed and then use 1 teaspoon per cup of tea. Don't drink and drive!

Hot Flashes (Rosemary's Advice)

Try drinking 4-5 cups of sage tea every day. When I started getting hot flashes, I went back to Rosemary's lesson books and found that several women had reported that sage tea helped them. I gave it a try and it definitely helped me sleep better at night, *and* it lessened the severity of my hot flashes. In fact, once I discovered sage tea, I stopped having to change my clothes five times a day. If you can't put your hands on the dried herb, sage tea is readily available in your local health food store.

Rosemary also suggests taking 2 ginseng tablets twice a day. Ginseng helps the body combat stress and fatigue and is excellent for long-term imbalances, i.e., the hormone imbalances that are part of menopause. Ginseng also helps with mood swings and depression.

Stress

My "day job" is very stressful and when it gets crazy, a couple of sprays of Bach Rescue Remedy really help me keep it together. I keep Bach Rescue Remedy Spray in my pocketbook, and I have been known to give bottles of it to my friends and fellow managers when their stress levels increase for personal and/or business reasons. I even gave some to my husband when he decided to start his own business from home. Truth to tell, I gave myself a new bottle that day too—and anyone whose spouse works out of the house or is recently retired will understand why! Two sprays and the calming effects kicks right in.

I first read about Rescue Remedy in Rosemary's class materials, and it's easy to find in health food stores and on-line. Rescue Remedy was created over 60 years ago by Dr. Edward Bach, and there are 38 different Bach Flower Essences on the market although I've only personally used the Rescue Remedy. I like it because it's a natural method of healing (an infusion of spring water with wild flowers), and it helps restore the *balance* between mind and body, which, in my opinion, is the foundation of good health.

The Rescue Remedy contains five flower essences that work together for a calming effect: Rock Rose for terror and panic, Impatiens for irritation and impatience, Clematis for inattentiveness, Star of Bethlehem for shock and Cherry Plum for irrational thoughts. It has a very calming and centering energy.

As I was reviewing the flowers used in Rescue Remedy, I had an epiphany! Patience is an area I continue to struggle with, and so I went to the Bach website (www.bachflower.com) and found that they have an Impatiens Flower Essence! I laughed aloud when I read the description for it, and I have to share part of it with you:

> *For those who are quick in thought and action and who wish all things to be done without hesitation or delay...They find it very difficult to be patient with people who are slow as they consider it wrong and a waste of time, and they will endeavor to make such people quicker in all ways...*

I bet I can get my husband and co-workers to chip in and buy me a case!

One last note before I end this chapter—I recently discovered a new book that I have to share with you. It's called *The Enchanted Garden* by Jody Felice (available through www.Ozarkmt.com). Ms. Felice writes about how to use the energies of herbs, vegetables, and spices to "stimulate our emotions, motivate our minds, aid our physical bodies, and nurture our spirit.... the task of each recipe is to inspire you to connect with these powerful energies and allow them to enhance your ability to create positive change." I am over the moon with the discovery of a cookbook that speaks to the energy of the ingredients in a recipe. It all goes back to what Edgar Cayce said over 70 years ago—what we eat and the way we eat affects our health and well-being.

I hope you are moved to explore the intriguing and captivating world of traditional herbal medicine—and I especially hope that you will share your formulas and discoveries with your family and friends, and me, too. I know you'll have a line of people waiting for the burn salve!

Chapter Thirty-Six:

Naturopathy

What does naturopathy have to do with raising our vibrations? If we're balanced and healthy, we can draw and hold more light, and our output of positive energy will be higher.

Let's start this chapter with some additional wisdom and advice from Gilbert and the Group about treating dis-ease, which is a great segue into a discussion of naturopathy:

Dis-ease is brought about in several ways, and the treating of underlying cause(s) of the dis-ease is the action that should be taken. Covering symptoms may make the patient feel better temporarily, but if the cause is left untreated, the dis-ease will eventually return. For that reason, it is better to treat the whole person and not simply the complaint at hand. When you treat the whole person, you will not only find the source of the dis-ease, you will also enable the patient to work through blockages that are keeping them from moving forward vibrationally.

Naturopathy is a form of natural healing that is based on six principles: (1) let nature heal; (2) identify and treat causes; (3) first, do no harm; (4) educate patients; (5) treat the whole person; and (6) prevent illness. When you consider Gilbert's words in relation to the Six Principles of Naturopathy, it's easy to see why I was attracted to this area of study—it includes everything that's important to me with regard to healing. Here's a more comprehensive definition of naturopathy written by the American Association of Naturopathic Physicians:

> *Naturopathic medicine is based on the belief that the human body has an innate healing ability, and Naturopathic doctors (NDs) teach their patients to use diet, exercise, lifestyle changes and cutting edge natural therapies to enhance their bodies' ability to ward off and combat disease. Naturopathic medicine is based on the belief that the human body has an innate healing ability. NDs view the patient as a complex, interrelated system (a whole person), not as a clogged artery or a tumor. Naturopathic physicians craft comprehensive treatment plans that blend the best of modern medical science and traditional natural medical approaches to not only treat disease, but to also restore health.*

Following the positive experiences I had with herbology, I was very much moved to expand my horizons, and as I said earlier, naturopathy fit the bill for me.

Once I knew I wanted to study naturopathy, I needed to find a school, and in the early 90's my choices were limited. I was happy to find the Clayton College of Natural Healing and their distance learning program. Clayton College is certified as an Alternative and Continuing Education provider by the United States Distance Learning Association (USDLA), and as of this writing, continues to be "non-accredited." Accredited or non-accredited, I have to say that the distance learning curriculum at Clayton was as or more challenging than the classes I took to earn my A.A. and B.A. degrees from fully accredited colleges in New York State. It took me nearly two years of putting in 50-60 hours a month to complete my ND studies, and what I learned from Clayton, I learned for a reasonable amount of money. Because my goal was to "treat" only myself, the degree was secondary to me although it does look very nice on my wall! If you plan to open a practice, the subject of accreditation will be more important to you, and here are some choices to look into: the Boucher Institute of Naturopathic Medicine, the Canadian College of Naturopathic Medicine, and the South West College of Naturopathic Medicine. More and more facilities are offering studies in alternative medicine these days, so do a search on-line and see what's offered near you or check out the Clayton School.

I learned so much about such varied and interesting subjects while I was working on my ND degree. My curriculum included courses in herbology, nutrition, human anatomy, massage, acupressure, reflexology, iridology, arthritis, cancer, fasting, and homeopathy. So what did I learn? Well, if I had to boil down everything I learned down to one piece of advice it would be this: watch what you put inside your body. What we eat affects the balance of our body, and if our body isn't balanced, its ability to heal itself is diminished. I believe we can help our bodies get back on track and re-balance them naturally through proper diet, herbal remedies, and exercise.

SECTION TEN:

After the Shift

Chapter Thirty-Seven:

A Quick Review

Let's take a moment to review. In previous sections, we received advice to facilitate the Shift for ourselves, our fellow human beings, and for our beloved planet Earth. We know we're already experiencing the Shift although we don't know exactly when it will be complete, and we know that there will be challenges as we continue our evolutionary journey. We also know that we can temper the challenges by attracting, holding, and sharing the light on a global basis. We know that as Lightworkers, Starseeds, and citizens of this planet, the time is now to take action to help ourselves and each other through this momentous moment in universal history as we evolve to a new level of being. But what will things be like AFTER the Shift? In the following chapter, Gilbert and the Group give us "sneak peak" into what we can expect on New Earth after the Shift is complete.

Chapter Thirty-Eight:

Life on New Earth

This chapter includes any and all bits of dictation that mentions life on New Earth, presented in the order in which they were received during different sessions. Often the Guide Group would start writing about one subject, throw in a sentence or two about New Earth and then go back to their original subject, making it difficult to put together a cohesive chapter. For lack of a better idea, I'm presenting the New Earth tidbits here in the order in which they were received.

The New Earth will be the next stage in human evolution and the veil will be much thinner. There will be contact with those on the other side of the veil, and the upside of this is that no one will feel alone or mourn for home on a soul level or mourn those who pass over.

Let us address 'death' on the New Earth. There will be a passing over as there is now, but illness will not be the cause as there will be no sickness or disease. Those who transition and those who incarnate on the New Earth will have no need of karmic lessons since they will be awake and able to approach their learning in a way that is similar to taking classes and attending lectures on the other side of the veil. Human beings will transition back to the other side of the veil at will when their lessons are finished and their goals have been met. They will make that decision consciously and inform their families and friends who will not be sad as they will know they can still be in contact with the departing entity.

There will still be births immediately after the Shift, but that method of incarnating will eventually come to an end as human beings continue to grow and evolve.

Those who transition initially will feel a sense of wonder as they ease into their new bodies and begin to understand the power they have, especially with regard to the speed with which thoughts will be manifested. We told you in past writings that thoughts are becoming things much more quickly and that it is a must to watch your words and thoughts right now because they will quickly be manifested. As fast as you see this happening now on Planet Earth, it will be almost instantaneous on the New Earth. That is why it is a good thing to train yourself now to pay attention to your thoughts and words.

Organized religion will not exist on the New Earth. This is because all will be awake and able to communicate directly with their guides and loved ones on the other side of the veil.

Entities who transition to and enter the New Earth will have houses, food, and everything they want and need because they will be able to attain these things through apportation, meaning that they can call them into being through their own thought processes. It will take those who transition a little time to get used to doing things this way, but the Indigos, Crystals and Rainbows will be there to help ease the transition. These groups are wired for the New Earth more so than the Lightworkers and will be more adept at first when it comes to working with the energies and apportation.

Meditation will be a means of communication with one's Higher Self and also to connect with one's guides and those on the other side of the veil. The veil will be much more transparent than it is at the present time, and after the Shift, it will be possible to communicate directly from this side to that side and vice versa.

What will also be understood is that the Creator is not hands on, nor is the Creator a male or a female entity.

Human Beings will coexist without violence or fear, and that is a very big part of the New Earth, the ability to live and learn and grow without fear.

No one will have to wonder where his/her food is coming from. All will have sufficient shelter, and all will meet with like-minded entities to continue their growth and learning experiences. It will be a calm planet, the New Earth.

Now we wish to continue speaking about the New Earth and life there. Immediately after the Shift, you will find that entities will engage in occupations that reflect their interests from the Old Earth—they will do things that they always wanted to do but never had time to do, and they will also find they have talents they didn't realize they had when they were part of the third-dimensional energy of Old Earth.

The human race will find that that which they wish to learn and master, will come easily because fifth-dimensional entities can draw on all of their talents, whereas entities struggling to learn in a third-dimensional density suppress their talents for the purpose of growth. Currently, incarnated entities must "forget" who they are and what they know in order to concentrate on the lessons before them—that is where their focus and concentration must be in order to progress. All entities, when they are on this side of the veil, are accomplished in song and dance if they choose to be so. Entities on this side of the veil can create things from the thoughts in their heads—what

241

they think becomes real. After the Shift is complete, human beings will carry this knowledge and these abilities with them when they are in body.

Let us continue our work this morning and talk of the new age and what things will be like for the inhabitants of the New Earth. The New Earth will be a place of great beauty, and the people who make the transition will be beyond violence so it will be a planet of peace.

These newly evolved souls will have a mission. As the first inhabitants, they take on roles akin to that of architects and engineers as they assist in creating the blueprints for the planet and laying the foundation for the progressive planet that it will become.

The topography will be there, of course, and it will be very similar to this Earth plane, but it will be a little bit different—brighter if that makes sense to you.

The first transitioners will create the new societal norms, but they will be beyond the karmic wheel— that will be finished for them, and they will live very long lives. Eventually, they will not give birth and die the way humankind currently does—eventually souls will be able to come in through the light and leave through the light without the pain and drama. The work is what will be important.

So what will you find when the Shift is complete? You will find that your bodies will be much lighter than they are now and that you can move around and travel with ease. Eventually there will not be any need for vehicles because you will learn to apport yourselves where you want to be. The colors will be different because they will be seen as they truly are and not through a third-dimensional haze. There is a film or a fog on the present planet that you all look

242

through, and it keeps you from seeing things as they really are. That will not be the case on the New Earth, and things will appear to be brighter. And you will discover new colors because the spectrum will be seen in its entirety, not just the five colors you see now, and that will open up new color combinations for all to enjoy.

The above grouping of morsels from Gilbert and the Group provides us with a little glimpse into what awaits the first *transitioners* to New Earth. I love just the *thought* of peace on Earth. I have to share with you that I re-read this chapter over and over again, especially after I read or see something on TV about terrorist attacks and similar atrocities and skirmishes. It makes me feel better to know that peace is possible and very much in our future. I missed the whole 60s movement by just a few years—I was born in 1957, but I caught the tail end of it. I still give people the peace sign, and when I have a piece of paper sitting in front of me and I start to doodle, I draw the same things over and over again: the peace sign, pyramids, and of course, "the family cat." I don't think the family cat picture has any significance—it's just the only thing a person with my current limited artistic talent can draw, and it's called "family cat" because it's something Mom used to draw for all us kids, and we, in turn, would "master" drawing it for her. And I'm sure all who have heard me sing karaoke will be happy to learn that I'll finally be able to sing on key after the Shift is complete!

Let's talk about the term *light body* again. My understanding of this term is that our bodies will eventually be less physical and more energy-based after the shift to the fifth dimension is complete. With a *light body*, we will be able to see, sense, and feel the energies of the higher dimension and make them part of our daily lives. This is how we'll be able to apport and why our thoughts will manifest much more quickly.

The piece about seeing colors differently isn't new information—I've read this before in several books, and I've always had a hard time imagining new colors and what they will look like and be called. But it's fun to think about, isn't it? I've tried to picture new colors in my mind, but I can't do it—can you? Peace and new colors sound very cool, but the part that really got my attention was that there will be no karma to deal with on New Earth. How freeing is that—for the entities that transition and incarnate to be able to devote their much longer lives to joyful learning experiences without having to worry about karmic debt. This change will affect our planning sessions for future incarnations, too. We won't be spending time deciding or having to plan out what karma to deal with or having to create Windows of Opportunity to take care of it, and so I asked "What will be our planning sessions be like?" The answer was that they will be "mission-based" since those who transition and incarnate on New Earth will be awake with regard to what they are there to do. This is all so different from what we're used to but exhilarating to think about, don't you think?

I needed some clarification on the part about the way we will experience birth and death. No more pain and grief sounds great, but what about families? Without birth, will we still have families? And so I asked Gilbert to elaborate.

Sherri, there will be entities who will form groups to live together and work together, and there will be a camaraderie and a feeling of family. There will be those who do wish to combine their energies and form a family of sorts, but marriage, as you know it, will not be necessary or something that is done.

When an entity incarnates, it won't be in a body like you are used to having. It will be a lighter body, a body made of light and energy, and entities will enter as adults, not as babies or as children. The entities that incarnate will come in knowing and understanding their mission as they will be awake to who they are. Much progress will be made quickly this way.

Incarnations on New Earth will not be karma-based; the duality will be gone. Life will be mission-based, and when a group requires assistance or reaches a level where additional entities are needed, the correct entity for the mission will apport. All who come to the New Earth will have specific jobs to do and will understand their part in the overall mission at hand.

The thing to remember here, Sherri, is that the old paradigm of the family will not be necessary anymore because birth and infancy and childhood will be phased out as the inhabitants of New Earth continue to evolve.

It's hard to imagine a time when we aren't bogged down by karma, isn't it? And it makes sense that our culture will change completely when we don't have to deal with such things. Oh, I looked up "apport" and "apportation." They mean "the carrying or projecting of an object through space, whether a human form or any other thing." I guess that makes sense—entities will be moving from one space or dimension into another. Now there's a cool new (or remembered) skill that we can all look forward to having in future lifetimes—the ability to apport the things we want instead of having to go to the mall or the grocery store! Let's get back to more of what we can expect after the Shift.

Initially, life on the New Earth will be similar to Old Earth in that there will be houses, farms, cities, and whatever the first arrivals decide to construct. The main difference from life on Old Earth is that life will be more joyous and peaceful.

Food sources will change as, of course, all will be vegetarian and all will eat fruit and plant sources of nutrition. And no one will care. They will be satisfied with the food. There will be no hunting and no violence because that is not the way of a fifth-dimensional being. When individuals ascend to this level, it is because their vibrational level is in synch with the frequency of the planet, and no one who ascends to this level would involve themselves in violence.

Human beings will take their place as part of the galactic family and begin to participate in galactic conferences as they become fully aware of other fifth-dimensional species. Interaction with other species will begin to take place and become commonplace as evolution continues.

It is such a magnificent thing that is happening and many want to watch this experiment come to fruition. That is why you are being watched as if you are on a big screen TV with the signal emanating throughout the galaxy. There are some groups of beings who don't believe it will happen—they think that the human life form will not be able to pull it off and that at the end of the day they will retreat back to their place of duality and negative thoughts—and stay for another millennium. But they are wrong. There will be those who stay, of course, because they are not ready to make the Shift, but the planet is going to make the Shift and human beings will evolve the next level.

With regard to the food supply, well, all who make the change with the planet will become vegetarian, whether they are so in this current incarnation or not. There will be no killing of animals for food. The time of ingesting animals or animal products will be past— there will be no need for it, and your new bodies will not be able to ingest or digest that kind of fear-based

246

energy. The first wave of transitioners will eat vegetables and fruits, which they will grow, and the flavors and tastes will be astonishing to them. An apple will be an apple, but it will look more red or green because of the difference in colors that will be encountered, and the taste will still be apple-y but more so.

Vegetarianism, of course, will be the new way of consuming food, and food will be provided on the New Earth through farming methods that are unlike the ones currently in use. Farming will be a much easier occupation because there will not be any interference from bad weather or catastrophes like bugs eating the crops. Food will be grown. Period. And it will be distributed properly, meaning that no one will ever go hungry on the New Earth. There will be plenty of food, and no one country or continent will have any more or less than another. There will be equality in food resources, and, therefore, there will be nothing to fight over in that regard.

There will be vehicles although they are not really needed, but the first wave will want them because they will feel familiar. As life goes on, over time there will be less of that kind of thing because all who are there will be able to simply think themselves where they want to be. They will be powered through telekinesis. Because there will be no need to have oil or gasoline to power vehicles, there will be no reason for countries to fight over what used to be considered valuable resources.

People will still have occupations, but they will be able to do the things they want to do, things that help to further increase the vibrational level of the human race and the planet and enable them to become galactically acclimated. They will continue to evolve as a species.

The temperature will always be comfortable, no freezing temperatures and no high temperatures that will melt you like butter, yet you will still be able to go skiing if you want to. You will able to think it and then experience it, but you won't need a parka to keep you warm and comfortable going down the slopes! These things sound far-fetched to you, we know, but this is the way of the New Earth.

We wish to speak to you about government as that is something that will change greatly on the New Earth. A rudimentary government will try to form, but it won't be needed because of the level of communication that will exist at that time. When human beings reclaim their power of being able to communicate telepathically with each other, there will little need for Congress and Senate as the feelings of the people will be known by everyone. Quorums will be reached easily, and the people will govern themselves although there will be ambassadors and emissaries. As in the lack of religious groups that will be found, so will there be a lack of governmental interference because it simply won't be necessary.

And that is everything I received from the Gilbert and the Group about what we can expect on New Earth following the transition. As soon as the Group started using the term, New Earth, I felt like it was familiar, and a couple of weeks later, Heidi Winkler mentioned that Dolores Cannon used the same phrase in *The Convoluted Universe, Book Two* and in Eckhart Tolles' *The New Earth*. I immediately pulled out my copy of Dolores' book, and with her permission, here are some excerpts from Convoluted Universe that describe some of what we can expect to find on New Earth:

- This is a quote from Dolores: "...*I have been told that the Earth itself is changing its vibration and frequency, and it is preparing to raise itself into a new dimension. There are countless dimensions surrounding us all the time. We cannot see them because as the vibration speeds up, they are invisible to our eyes, but they still exist, nonetheless.*" This is very similar to the information dictated by Gilbert and the Group, and also to the information I researched about parallel universes.

- In talking about the physical body as its vibrational level increases, Dolores wrote: *With the changes subtly going on around us, our physical bodies must also change in order to adjust...our bodies must become lighter, and this means the elimination of heavy foods. During my sessions, my clients are repeatedly warned to stop eating meat, mainly because of the additives and chemicals that are being fed to animals...it is very difficult to eliminate these toxins from the body. . . The body cannot ascend in frequency to higher dimensional realms if the density and the toxins are polluting the environment of the human body.*

This confirms why Gilbert and the Group wanted this book to contain sections about vegetarianism, herbalism, and naturopathy. It's important to recognize that we are already in the process of evolving into our *light bodies*, and it's time to change our eating habits to ease this transition.

My gut tells me that while it's fun to hear and read about what New Earth will be like, it's much more important to take care of the business of the here and now—which means taking care of ourselves, both physically and spiritually. We can make a lot of progress over time if we start with small steps, like making changes in our dietary habits, meditating on a regular basis, and smiling and being nicer to each other. These changes will help us absorb more light, be better prepared for the transition, and we'll make Old Earth a better place for those who remain.

SECTION ELEVEN:

Opening Up to Spirit

Chapter Thirty-Nine:

Meditation

Meditation is a state of awareness; and the word "meditation" has its roots in Latin and means "to think" and "to heal." I am not shy when it comes to suggesting to folks that they give meditation a try. I believe wholeheartedly that meditation is a tool that has both physical and spiritual benefits, including increasing our personal power and our vibrational levels. It's a tool that's always within reach whenever we need it, and it assists us in achieving results on several levels, including (but certainly not limited to) the following:

- **Learning to focus our attention inward.** The benefits of doing this are these: (1) an improved ability to relax; (2) an inner calm that allows us to stop sweating the little things and to put them into perspective; and (3) an increased ability to resolve problems through a more developed and deeper insight, which leads to accessing the creative centers of our mind.

- **Healing our bodies and spirit through concentrated awareness.** This will allow us to release pent-up or misplaced anger, ease stress, deal with grief, and face our fears—all of which lends itself to increased vibrational levels. The practice of "following your breath" (being aware of each inhalation and exhalation) during meditation teaches and allows us to practice proper breathing, which leads to better health. Proper breathing allows us to bring our bodies and minds into harmony on all levels. [Note: You'll find some information about proper breathing a little further into this chapter.]

- **Getting to know our true selves.** Yes, meditation provides ongoing opportunities for us to get to know ourselves better, tap into and better hear our inner guidance (Higher Self), and attain an open and calm mindset that facilitates direct contact with our spirit guides and angels.

From where I sit, the hardest thing about meditation is getting started because once you have a few sessions under your belt, you'll be a believer in daily meditation. It restores balance to your body and your mind, and it's better than taking a power nap! Start with five minutes and work your way up to 20 or 30 minutes a day. Here are some simple, basic steps to help you get started, followed by a breathing meditation exercise.

Meditation Basics

- Pick a time of day when you can sit in undisturbed silence for at least 15-20 minutes.

- Try to meditate at the same time each day.

- Sit upright in a comfortable chair or lay down on the floor or the couch; do whatever feels comfortable to you.

- If you want to burn a candle and/or incense, go ahead.

- Close your eyes and start to clear your mind.

- As thoughts come in, don't worry about it. Just recognize them and send them away. You can think about those things later!

- Sit quietly for 15 – 20 minutes—set a timer if you want to.

- When you're finished meditating, remember to blow out candles and incense if you used them!

Breathing Meditation Exercise

- Sit quietly on the floor or on a chair, making sure that your back is straight and your spine is erect. Your hands can be folded together on your lap or resting palms up on your knees.

- Become aware of your body being supported by the earth and allow this awareness to enter and permeate your body.

- Begin to follow your breath as you inhale deeply and exhale fully. Feel yourself open up to the sensation and the power of your breath as you consciously begin to watch your breath and become more and more aware of your inhalations and exhalations.

- As you inhale, notice the temperature and the feeling of the air as you draw it in through your nose, then down through your throat, and finally, into your lungs. Feel the sensation of your belly expanding like a party balloon being filled with air.

- As you exhale, pay attention as you draw your breath from your lungs up and out through your throat and nose. Feel your belly flatten as you exhale.

- Continue to breathe this way and pay attention to your breath for five to ten minutes.

- When you're finished, sit still for a few minutes as you begin to pay attention to the way your body feels—note any new sensations from the energy and light you've absorbed.

In *Windows of Opportunity*, the GG spoke about meditation, and I think it's appropriate to repeat some of their words here.

> *To connect with the Source, you must go deeper. For that to happen, there must be discipline to meditate at the same time each and every day and to give it the time and care that it needs. For goodness sake, Sherri, if people knew they would experience joy and happiness by giving up a lousy fifteen to thirty minutes a day, why would they not do so?*

Re-reading the GG's comment about connecting to the Source reminded me of something I recently read in a book called *Thirty Miracles in Thirty Days* by Irene Lucas. I met Irene when we were both speakers at the 2010 Transformations Conference, and we hit it off instantly. I was immediately drawn to her energy and light, and I had the instantaneous sense that we've had many incarnations together. I bought her book and read it from cover to cover on the plane ride home. Irene says: "Change your breath, change your life! If you can breathe, you can heal," and with Irene's permission, here is a breathing exercise from her book called *The Holy Breath*.

The Holy Breath

> *The Holy Breath is the Breath of Spirit, of God. Breathe in, and breathe in Spirit. Breathe in God. As deeply as you can, breathe in through your nose; then breathe out through your mouth. Breathe in as deeply and comfortably as you can from your diaphragm; breathe out as strongly as you are comfortably able. As you breathe in God, you are refreshed, renewed, revived, infused with Divine*

256

energies. Breath out other energies (thoughts, experiences, contacts, stress, emotions)—envision your exhaling breath on a track of Divine Light [with your] energies immediately blessed, transformed, [and] returned to the Universe as Divine Love.

Irene then incorporates the choice of a healing ray into the meditation. Each Master has a color/s associated with him or her, and by breathing in that color ray, you are able to connect with the energies of that Master. You can read more about this in her book. I think *The Holy Breath* is a great way to focus attention and meditate more deeply. I nearly fell into a meditative state when I was typing the description! As you begin to incorporate meditation into your daily routine, the first step is to find a time of day that works for you, and then find a quiet place where you can sit up straight and let the light begin to flow. A good time to consider is first thing in the morning while you're still between realms, which makes for an easier transition to a meditative state. I always start an automatic writing session with at least a few deep breaths and preferably with at least 5-10 minutes of meditation. The increased light and energy that proper breathing draws into the body helps me connect quickly and clearly with my Guides, Guide Groups, and other "visiting" entities.

If you're already meditating, I am giving you a standing ovation. If you haven't tried it yet or you're not meditating regularly, then let's make a pact to do so. Choose a time and place and meditate every day even if it's just for five or ten minutes. Do it every day for two weeks straight, and I promise you that you will be hooked for the rest of your life. Your life will be healthier, happier, and more serene because you are taking the time to use this spiritual growth tool that we all have at our fingertips. Meditation—try it. You'll like it!

Chapter Forty:

Automatic Writing

Since *Windows of Opportunity* came out at the end of 2009, I've received e-mails and letters from many individuals who decided to connect with their guides through automatic writing. It's such a joy and honor whenever someone shares his/her journey and automatic writing experiences with me. I am also honored when I hear from people like Lightworker Pam Bajaj of Woodland Hills, California, who, instead of sitting around feeling frustrated, took the time to shoot me an e-mail to ask if she was "doing it right." As I told Pam and everyone who wrote to me about this subject, there is no "right" or "wrong" way to do automatic writing—the *key* is to be patient and persistent. You can't give up if it doesn't happen the first time, second time, or even the third time that you try. It took me several months to make contact for the first time. I nearly gave up! Now look: I've taken dictation from Spirit for two books! Being comfortable and relaxed always helps, and after several tries and no connection, Lightworker and Reiki Master Shelly Wilson of Vinita, Oklahoma, wrote to say that when she moved to a different spot in her house where the sound of the A/C didn't distract her, she was finally able to connect.

Automatic writing is a form of channeling, and it's my channeling method of choice for a couple of reasons: (1) my memory is not what it used to be, and I like to have a written record of all personal messages; and (2) I *must* have a written record of all book dictation so that I can make sure that the messages you read from the Guide Group are exactly the way they were given to me. I really need to write everything down because I have a worse memory than I thought, an example of which I will share with you in just a moment. This is why even though I can clearly hear what's being said to me by Spirit during our book sessions, I insist on taking everything down on paper.

Do you remember when I told you about my first on-line meeting with Gilbert and about the snarky comment I made about his name? Well, I recently stumbled on some personal automatic writing with Jeremy that took place in July 2009, a full eight months before I started taking dictation for this book. I'm including it below not only because it shows why I write everything down (and note to self, you have to read the notes!), but also because I want you to see that conversations with your Guides are like conversations with your best friend.

Sherri: "Will someone write with me?"

Jeremy: *"Sherri, I am here."*

Sherri: "Did I just have a crazy dream last night, or is there someone named Gilbert about to dictate the next book?"

Jeremy: *"Sherri, you did not have a crazy dream. In fact, we made contact last night to try and get you to move along with the next book. We are late getting started. As to Gilbert, he is a wise and experienced guide who will assist in the dictating of book number two. You and Gilbert go back eons together, and he is ready to get moving with the new book."*

Sherri: "Why would I dream that I was attracted to him and be ditching Ted to be with him?"

Jeremy: *"Sherri, that's just the way the dream felt to you; sorry for unsettling you. It is time to light a fire under you, and you and Gilbert go back a long time—during the dream you recognized the energy, the vibrational feel, of Gilbert, and you were joyful for the reunion. There is much to do and much to say, and we will do it as we planned. Sherri, Gilbert wishes to write with you now."*

Gilbert: *"You are late! Let us move on with this project! Sherri, you and I have been together in many lifetimes and in between lifetimes. We will have fun working on this project together. I am psyched for it, and I hope you are, too."*

Sherri: "Okay...but I'm still trying to get book one out there, so doing book two seems crazy to me right now.

Gilbert: *"We have a group here on this side assigned to this project, and it is time for you and me and the group to move forward and get this project done. Go in peach[1] and get ready to rock and roll."*

---

[1] Note from Sherri: When I first switched from paper to the computer, the word "peace" came out "peach," as I was adjusting to the keyboard. Since then, it's become a running joke as my GG's end each session with the words "Go in peach."

And there you have it. How could I forget this encounter? I have no idea, except that I found it in a file filled with admonitions from Jeremy and the original GG to get off my butt and get to work on Book Two. What I hope you take from this sample is that communicating with your guides doesn't have to be a stuffy, formal interaction You know your guides well, and they want you to be relaxed and to ask lots of questions. And...if you happen to be working on a project together, they also want you to be on time!

Here's another reason I love automatic writing. Even though I'm in a slightly altered state of consciousness (thanks to deep breathing and meditation before I get started), I'm still wide awake and fully conscious while I'm taking the dictation or having the conversation. I know exactly what's being said/written, and I can stop the writing at any time to ask questions or request clarification. As you saw above, automatic writing is very much a "back and forth" method of communicating with your guides, angels, and friends and family on the other side. If you're ready to give automatic writing a try, here are some basic instructions to get you started.

- Choose a time of day when you can sit undisturbed for at least 15 minutes. Meditate first or do some deep breathing to help you relax.

- Sit comfortably with a pad of paper on the table in front of you and hold a pen or pencil loosely in your hand with the tip of your writing instrument touching the paper. You can use a computer keyboard instead of pad and paper.

- Say a prayer of protection; here's mine (My first teacher, Cyndi, gave this to me in 1987): *"I am protected by the love of God; only those entities*

262

of the highest intentions can pass through my door. If others should try, my door will immediately close, effectively blocking them out. This is my prayer of protection. Amen."

- Write on the top of the paper, "Will someone write with me?"

- Clear your mind and wait. If it helps you to burn incense or candles, go right ahead. Remember to blow them out when you're finished.

- If nothing happens within the first five minutes, end the session. It won't be happening that day.

Your First Connection

- When you first connect, it will feel like someone is grasping your hand and or your arm. Just relax—let it happen.

- You will most likely experience circles, figure 8's, and back and forth movements with your pen or pencil.

- Ask the entity for his or her name and ask the entity what his or her relationship is to you. Don't go any further until you start to write words, and you know who you're writing with.

- Next ask the entity for a message; i.e., "Do you have something to share with me?" Write this down on the paper and wait for a response. As you get information, you can ask questions about what you're receiving—just write them down and wait for the response.

- When you and/or your guide/s are finished, you'll feel the pen (or your hands if you're typing) relax. Be sure to thank your guide/s for working with you. After I say "thank you," or when my guides are finished, they generally write, "Go in Peace" to signify the end of a session. You'll establish a similar type of routine with your guide(s).

Continued Sessions

Always do your automatic writing at the same time each day. Just because an entity doesn't happen to be in a body, doesn't mean that he or she doesn't have things to do! Be respectful of your guide's/s' time. If you can't make a session, tell your guide/s you aren't coming that day. You can use paper and pen or your computer keyboard. ALWAYS say a prayer of protection before each session—it will keep you firmly in the light.

The paragraph you have just started reading is one of the most important paragraphs in this entire book, so pay attention! If you want to connect with Spirit through automatic writing, you **will** do it. It might take some time, but you **will** be able to do it. There is absolutely, positively, nothing special about me, or anyone else that channels spirit. Spirit is ready to communicate with you; no, Spirit is communicating with you right now. My chosen method is automatic writing, yours might be through information received during meditation, during your dream state, or while you're taking a shower or driving your car. The bottom line is this: Our Guides and Angels surround us with love and support and talk to us every day. They send messages through meditation, and our dreams, during automatic writing, through synchronistic events, and even via repeating numbers. We just have to wake ourselves up, pay attention to what's going on inside of us and around us, and we will get our messages. You know, this seems like a really good spot for a "knock-knock" joke, but I can't think of one!

SECTION TWELVE:

Ready for Action!

Chapter Forty-One:

Opening our Toolbox

In Chapter Nineteen (aptly titled "A New Way of Living") of her book, *I Can See Clearly Now,* Mary Soliel writes the following words that are both simple yet profoundly important for all of us on Planet Earth: "An evolution in the way we view and experience life begins with our awareness that we truly do create our lives." Whether we like it or not, we are evolving, and the burdens and joys of this evolution are firmly in our hands.

We decide what we will experience during our lifetimes and waking up to this knowledge and having the *awareness* that we create our lives, well, that is truly evolution. That's called "waking up" to who we really are, and with this knowledge and awareness comes responsibility. Did Eve take a bite of the apple and cause us to be kicked out of Eden and have to contend with bad things happening to us? Did Pandora open the box and release all the evils of the world on us? No, the actions of Eve and Pandora were not the deciding factors in what happens to us—we decide those things for ourselves, and we know what we're doing because we've had lifetimes of practice. But now with this lifetime, we are all grown up. We're not children when it comes to the art of a successful incarnation, and many of us are warriors on the battlefield of evolution.

Evolving is like a battle, and I'm reminded of Robert Frost's poem, "The Road Not Taken." We have choice, and what road will we choose? The road where we are blind and blame others for our trials and tragedies or the road where we are awake and turn those trials and tragedies into triumphs of learning and spiritual growth?

Once we "taste the apple" and know in our hearts that there is "something more" than blindly following the crowd, we have to choose whether to pretend to be blind or to boldly go where humankind has never gone before. By firmly taking the reins, by taking responsibility for ourselves and our planet, we will use our considerable power to expedite our spiritual growth, *and* we will spare ourselves much drama and pain as we become better and better at taking charge of our lives and our growth.

The goals of Jeremy, Gilbert, Akhnanda, Olexeoporath, and all the other guides and entities who participated in putting this book together are simple: to give us the understanding of who we are and to remind us about the tools we have at our disposal to make this incarnation and this evolutionary step easier for us and for our planet. Whether we are transitioning to the fifth dimension or staying to finish important business in the third, we have the power individually and collectively to make things better for all human beings. They've done their part, and now it's time for us to do ours. It's time to open our collective toolboxes, get to work, and celebrate the ever-evolving story of *us*.

Books, Articles, & Websites Quoted/Mentioned In "Raising Our Vibrations for the New Age"

Books:

"The Convoluted Universe" series by Dolores Cannon
"Children of the Stars" by Nikki Patillo
"A Spiritual Evolution" by Nikki Patillo
"I Can See Clearly Now—how Synchronicity Illuminates our Lives" by Mary Soliel
"Thirty Miracles in Thirty Days" by Irene Lucas
"Phoenix Star" by Kiernan Antares
"Herbal Healing for Women" by Rosemary Gladstar
"Gladstar Family Herbal" by Rosemary Gladstar
"The Enchanted Garden" by Jody Felice
"A Lightworker's Way" by Doreen Virtue
"Angel Numbers" by Doreen Virtue
"Crystal Enlightenment" by Katrina Raphaell
"Crystal Healing" by Katrina Raphaell
"The Crystalline Transmission" by Katrina Raphael
"The Game of Life" by Florence Scovel Shinn
"Your Word is Your Wand" by Florence Scovel Shinn
"The Power of the Spoken Word" by Florence Scovel Shinn
"The Secret Door to Success" by Florence Scovel Shinn
"The Intenders Handbook, a Guide to the Intention Process and the Conscious Community" by Tony Burroughs
"New Spiritual Technology for Fifth Dimensional Earth" by David K. Miller
"The Celestine Prophecy" by James Redfield
"Edgar Cayce on Atlantis" by ??????????
"Edgar Cayce on Healing" by Mary Ellen Carter & William A. McGarey

"Exploring Atlantis" books 1-3 by Frank Alper
"The Vital Energy of Movement: The Secret of 2012" by Jorge
    Baez
"Communion" by Whitley Strieber
"Transformation" by Whitley Strieber
"The Prism of Lyra" by Lyssa Royal & Keith Priest
"Pleiadian Perspectives on Human Evolution" by Amora
    Quan Yi
"The Pleiadian Workbook" by Amora Quan Yi
"All I Really Need to Know I Learned in Kindergarten" by
    Robert Fulghum
"Moldavite: Starborn Stone of Transformation" by Robert
    Simmons and Kathy Warner
"Eating Animals" by Jonathan Safran Foer
"The New Earth" by Eckhart Tolles

Articles/Websites:

www.angeltherapy.com (Doreen Virtue)
www.truthbrigaderadio.com (Christie Czajkowski)
www.angelicchanneler.com (Jeanne Barnes)
www.hubpages.com (Lots of articles by many authors)
www.spiritualgrowth.com (Lots of articles by many authors)
www.ezines.com (lots of articles by many authors)
www.**wellness**downtown.com (New World Wellness,
    Kissimmee, FL)
www.freetobemespa.com (Free To Be Me Wellness Spa &
    Salon, Bloomingdale, IL)
www.studiokyoga.com (Studio K Yoga, Kissimmee, FL)
www.shellywilson.com (Reiki Master/Intuitive)
www.heavenandearthjewelry.com (moldavite)
www.edgarcayce.org (Association for Research &
    Enlightenment, aka "A.R.E.)
www.bachflower.com (Rescue Remedy and Bach Flower
    Remedies)

www.sagemt.com (Herbal home study course with Rosemary Gladstar)

www.drugs.com (Information about various drugs)

www.huffingtonpost.com (Article: "Eating Animals: Why Eating Matters" by Kathy Freston)

www.spiritualnetwork.net/chakra (Chakra info)

www.Kryon.com ("The Doom Factory" article by Lee Carroll)

www.blogtalk**radio**.com/**heaven-knows** (Mary Soliel)

http://www.legendarytimes.com (Giorgio A. Tsoukalos) This website also includes information about the History Channel's 4-part series "Ancient Aliens."

www.science.howstuffworks.com/paralleluniverse1.htm (Article: "Do Parallel Universes Really Exist" article by Josh Clark

http://science.howstuffworks.com/quantum-suicide3.htm (Article about Quatum Suicide by Josh Clark)

www.tentmaker.org/articles/if**hell**isreal.htm (Article: "Honest Questions and Answers about Hell" by Mercy Aiken & Gary Amirault)

www.bocaburger.com (vegetarian food products)

www.morninstarfarms.com (vegetarian food products)

www.quorn.com (vegetarian food products)

www.amyskitchen.com (vegetarian food products)

www.organic-food-for-everyone.com (Definition of "organic food")

Sherri Cortland, ND

Sherri has always had an unquenchable thirst for all things metaphysical. As a child, she frequently raided her mother's bookshelf for any and all books about reincarnation, karma, numerology, and life after death. A friend introduced her to Shirley MacLaine's *Out on a Limb* when it first came out in 1983, and that was it. She was off on her own personal search for truth! After reading others' information, she decided she wanted to obtain great wisdom and knowledge directly, so she started studying automatic writing as a way to connect with the other side.

While simultaneously working on her B.A. in Communications and taking psychic development classes in the late 80's, Sherri made *first contact* with her guides through automatic writing. Always a lifelong learner, Sherri then studied herbology with Rosemany Gladstar (1993) and earned a Doctor of Naturopathy degree from Clayton College of Natural Health in 1998.

Since 1987, Sherri has been communicating with Jeremy and other guides, each with his/her own personality, wisdom, and information. Her go-to-Guide, Jeremy, led the Guide Group that channeled information for her first book, *Windows of Opportunity*. Guides Gilbert and Akhnanda and their respective groups started working with Sherri in 2009 and 2010 and provided the channeled information found in *Raising Our Vibrations for the New Age.*

Originally from New York State, Sherri currently resides in Orlando, Florida, with her husband, Ted Dylewski. Sherri's "Day Job" is Director of Specialty Sales for Westgate Resorts in Orlando, Florida, where she writes and teaches sales training workshops and customer service classes for sales professionals and sales support staff.

She is currently working on her third book, tentatively titled, "Spiritual Toolkit." Sherri can be reached through www.SherriCortland.com or www.FaceBook.com/SherriCortland